Kevin,

Thank you for everything that you have done for the venture world. You are a source of inspiration to all of us. Hope you enjoy reading this book which I am launching this month. Wishing you all the success and health.

Best,

Praise for *Selling Your Startup*

"Don't sell your business until you've read this book. *Selling Your Startup* is an essential resource founders have needed for a long time. The world is awash with advice on *how* to *start* a business, but Cremades shares practical wisdom on how to play the end game."

—Will Glaser, Cofounder
Sold Pandora to SiriusXM for $3.5 billion

"If you thought product market fit, fundraising, and scaling your startup were challenging, M&A will make those efforts look simple. Alejandro perfectly balances both the science and art of M&A from the sell side for entrepreneurs in this book, bringing clarity to what can feel like an extremely complex process. If you're a founder or entrepreneur, add this to your must-read list."

—Reggie Aggarwal, Cofounder
Sold Cvent to Vista Equity Partners for $1.65 billion

"Securing the right acquirer for your business, on the right terms, makes all of the difference in your vision being realized, or it being stolen and crushed. Use this resource to get clarity on your ideal target buyers and optimize the terms for lasting success."

—Kevin O'Connor, Cofounder
Sold DoubleClick to Hellman & Friedman for $1.1 billion

"The multiples your investment in reading this book can deliver are off the charts. Beyond the difference in financial outcome it may have, it could make all the difference in what happens to your company and customers next, and the opportunities you will have as an exiting founder."

—Duke Rohlen, Cofounder
Sold FoxHollow Technologies to Ev3 for $780 million

"I know of countless startups who could have benefited from the advice that Alejandro has collated here. I'm happy that this book now exists, so I can recommend it in the future to companies going through the stressful and often uncertain M&A process."

—Jack Smith, Cofounder
Sold Vungle to Blackstone for $750 million

"This is an essential guide for all founders. From surviving due diligence to maximizing price and terms, to getting through the emotional roller coaster, not killing your own deal, and setting up a great new chapter in your life, put this book on top of your reading list."

—Sandeep Akkaraju, CEO
Sold IntelliSense to Corning for $750 million

"I've cofounded and sold a number of companies in my career in the tech industry. It's always important to have great advice and counsel as you make these key transformative decisions. Alejandro's insight will help you develop better strategy and tactics to ace this pivotal part of the journey and get the most out of the opportunities and companies you create."

—Drew Perkins, Cofounder
Sold Lightera Networks to Ciena for $550 million

"You've put so much into starting a company you owe it to yourself to make sure the outcome is worth it. This book will help you make the most of your exit, no matter what the circumstances of selling your business are. From now on, I'll be recommending *Selling Your Startup* to every entrepreneur I meet."

—Will Herman, Cofounder
Sold ViewLogic to Synopsys for $497 million

"As you build your company and the various critical aspects—fundraising, which investors, culture, product market fit, and scale—put thought into what a successful exit looks like, as this does influence your success. This book will provide you information that can help you in your startup journey."

—Sujai Hajela, Cofounder
Sold Mist Systems to Juniper Networks for $405 million

"Once again Alejandro Cremades brings an incredible amount of much-needed knowledge to the startup community with this work of literature. This book is extremely useful to all companies and contains viable information that can set the stage for a successful M&A. No entrepreneur should be entertaining acquisition offers or even running a fundraising process until they've read this book."

—Lior Elazary, Cofounder
Sold EdgeCast to Verizon for $400 million

"*Selling Your Startup* is a must-read for all founders of funded startups. It is a credible resource that will help prepare entrepreneurs to skillfully navigate this often precarious part of the business cycle."

—Milind Mehere, Cofounder
Sold Yodle to Web.com for $340 million

"While every M&A situation is unique, many fundamentals are universally applicable. In *Selling Your Startup*, Alejandro Cremades breaks an often complex process down to the basics in a way that's both accessible and logical. Whether you're new to the world of M&A or simply looking to refresh your knowledge, this book is an invaluable read."

—Jeffrey Glass, Cofounder
Sold m-Qube to VeriSign for $250 million

"All great projects and startups begin with the end in mind. If your venture is a success, an exit is most definitely in your future. *Selling Your Startup* is a fantastic resource that the startup community has needed for a long time."

—Craig Walker, Cofounder
Sold GrandCentral to Google for $100 million

"Selling a startup is the most important decision in the life of an entrepreneur. I wish we had a book like this when we were in the process of selling our company."

—Ander Michelena, Cofounder
Sold Ticketbis to eBay for $190 million

"A startup is a very hard journey for any soul on this planet. Very very few startups get to IPOs and most need to get to a solid exit. Alejandro is demystifying the exit by giving everyone a cheat sheet to get the most from their hardships."

—Ramu Sunkara, Cofounder
Sold Qik to Skype for $150 million

"If you have done it right, so much time, energy, sweat, tears, and sacrifice go into creating and building a startup, so it's a tragedy when the outcome falls so far short of its potential because founders simply aren't prepared for this phase. This book finally turns the tables in favor of founders. No matter where you are in your startup, read this and know Alejandro has your back."

—Dane Madsen, Cofounder
Sold YellowPages for $100 million

"It's what you don't know that really hurts you in business. Until now, startup founders have been at an extreme disadvantage without access to this information. You owe it to yourself, your team, your investors, and customers to get equipped with this knowledge."

—Iñaki Berenguer, Cofounder
Sold Pixable to SingTel for $26 million and CoverWallet to Aon for an undisclosed amount

"A lot has been written about how to build and scale startups, but not about the process of selling them. Alejandro has compiled the collective wisdom of hundreds of the top founders with big exits and brings it altogether in this really one-of-a-kind book that is of immense value if you are ever going through this process."

—Luis Sanz, Cofounder
Sold Olapic to Monotype for $130 million

"*Selling Your Startup* is a must-read for the entrepreneur who needs to know the ins and outs of selling your business in the shark-infested waters of M&A. Alejandro's book provides you with the knowledge and insight you need to ensure you make the right decisions and optimize your opportunity. The emotional ups and downs of the process can be overwhelming so the key is to understand all your options throughout the process and plan your responses in advance so logic will prevail rather than the emotion of the moment."

—Allan Hahn, Founder
Sold multiple companies for $1 billion+

"Startup founders suffer from a basic disadvantage when selling their startups. For most, it is the first time they're going through that process, while everyone else involved (corporate buyers, investors, lawyers) have repeated experience at the art of M&A. With this book, Alejandro is tipping back the scale and demystifying this process in a clear, down-to-earth, and detailed language. Highly recommended reading for startup founders and execs."

—Eran Shir, Cofounder
Sold Dapper to Yahoo for $55 million

SELLING YOUR STARTUP

CRAFTING THE PERFECT EXIT, SELLING YOUR BUSINESS, AND EVERYTHING ELSE ENTREPRENEURS NEED TO KNOW

SELLING YOUR STARTUP

ALEJANDRO CREMADES

FOREWORD BY **BHAVIN TURAKHIA**

WILEY

Published by John Wiley & Sons, Inc., Hoboken, New Jersey.
Published simultaneously in Canada.

For general information on our other products and services or for technical support, please contact our Customer Care Department within the United States at (800) 762-2974, outside the United States at (317) 572-3993 or fax (317) 572-4002.

Wiley publishes in a variety of print and electronic formats and by print-on-demand. Some material included with standard print versions of this book may not be included in e-books or in print-on-demand. If this book refers to media such as a CD or DVD that is not included in the version you purchased, you may download this material at http://booksupport.wiley.com. For more information about Wiley products, visit www.wiley.com.

Library of Congress Cataloging-in-Publication Data

Names: Cremades, Alejandro, author.
Title: Selling your startup : crafting the perfect exit, selling your business, and everything else entrepreneurs need to know / Alejandro Cremades.
Description: Hoboken, New Jersey : Wiley, [2021] | Includes index.
Identifiers: LCCN 2021021825 (print) | LCCN 2021021826 (ebook) | ISBN 9781119797982 (hardback) | ISBN 9781119798057 (adobe pdf) | ISBN 9781119798040 (epub)
Subjects: LCSH: Sale of business enterprises. | New business enterprises.
Classification: LCC HD1393.25 .C74 2021 (print) | LCC HD1393.25 (ebook) | DDC 658.1/64–dc23
LC record available at https://lccn.loc.gov/2021021825
LC ebook record available at https://lccn.loc.gov/2021021826

Cover design and image: Wiley

SKY10027492 061121

To my love and life partner, Tanya, and my daughters, Mila, Liv, and Alya, the greatest joys of my life.

Contents

Acknowledgments

This book would have not been possible without the love and support of my wife, Tanya. She has always been there for me through the ups and downs of being an entrepreneur. Without a strong and supportive partner, it is impossible to take the leap of faith and build something from the ground up. The way she handled some of the most challenging events that came our way has been a constant source of inspiration for me. I wish all entrepreneurs had someone like Tanya by their side to help them keep pushing even during the darkest days of entrepreneurship when it is most needed.

I would also like to thank my little daughters, Mila, Liv, and Alya. At the time of writing this book, Mila was four years old and Liv and Alya were three years old. Even though they wanted to play at all times, they were very understanding when Daddy needed to work. Girls, if you ever read this, know that seeing you grow into intelligent, strong, and compassionate young women has been the best part of my life and a great motivation. More than anyone else, you are the people that I want to make proud of me.

Thank you to my father, Bernardo Cremades, my mother, Leticia Roman, and my brother, Bernardo Cremades Jr. They have always been rooting for me no matter what since the very early beginnings of my entrepreneurial journey. They have been constantly reliable and picked up the phone whenever I would call them even if it was 1:00 in the morning.

Furthermore, I would like to thank my father-in-law, Robert Shereck, and my mother-in-law, Gisele Prive. In addition to their love and support, they have taught me some of the biggest leadership lessons.

Other family members who have been very supportive through my journey are Carmen Posadas, Evan Prive, Zack Prive, and Beatriz Larrea.

This book would have never made it here without my publisher, Wiley. Especially Zach Schisgal. He has been a joy to work with and the person who believed in this book when I pitched him the idea.

One special person that has always been there for me is my other half in business, Michael Seversen. He came into my life at a point of transition after the acquisition of my previous company. Since then we have been business partners and we've had each other's back. There are no words to describe my gratitude to and appreciation of him.

Moreover, I would like to thank other members of my team for their help: Saroj Aggarwal, Miles Carter, Bryan Epstein, Vimal Gerda, Sri Gunasekaran, Tim Houghten, Zachary Jameson, Russell Michelson, Susan Nichols, Collin Robert, Prashant Sharma, Deepak Thakur, and Kammy Wood.

I would also like to thank all the people who have been involved with my prior ventures: investors, advisors, employees, and customers. Most of my knowledge about acquisitions comes as a result of working closely with you.

Last but not least, I want to offer my thanks to all of my readers. I appreciate the faith you are placing in me by reading my book, and I hope my experience and insights will help you forge your best path forward on your journey of selling your startup.

Thank you all. I am very fortunate to have you in my life.

Foreword
by Bhavin Turakhia

I believe it is our moral obligation to make an impact that is proportionate to our potential.

I have always had a passion for reading books and credit a lot to this habit inculcated into me during my early childhood. Reading enables you to shape your life from the wisdom and experiences of others. Stand on the shoulders of giants.

Growing up, I was a quintessential nerd—with a penchant for math and physics and a natural affinity for writing code from the age of 10. I was fortunate to find my passion early on and spent every spare moment in the computer room, when PCs were monochrome terminals with MS-DOS and 5¼-inch floppy drives. I devoured biographies with fervor and learnt much from the success and failures of Intel, Apple, Microsoft, Oracle, and countless others. It was clear to me then—I wanted to start my own company in this revolutionary new world.

Seven years later, I was raring to go, and along with my younger brother Div and $300 of borrowed capital from Dad, we started our first company—Directi—a web presence provider and domain name registrar.

Fourteen years later, we were number four worldwide, with 10 million domain names, a network of over 50,000 global resellers, and $70 million in revenues. Hari, then CEO of Endurance International and now a close family friend, approached us with an offer to buy Directi and I still remember to this day being very conflicted about it. However after six months of them courting us, and several deep strategic discussions, it made sense and we sold the company for $160 million—our first exit.

Div, my brother, had already independently started Media.net, which he then grew into a $900 million exit. And I had turned my attention to Radix (currently the number one new gTLD registry) and Flock (now Nova—competing with G Suite and Office and providing collaboration and productivity software to global users). Finally in 2015, I cofounded Zeta with Ramki Gaddipati—with a mission to make payments invisible and reimagine banking

I have never started any company with the goal of selling it. My startups were born out of my passions. I believe "frustration is the genesis of entrepreneurship"—and when entrepreneurs see something they would like to change, they go ahead and effectuate that change. If you are reading this book, perhaps you have already launched and built your own company or are in the process of starting up. As a successful business, however, most founders will receive one or more (bittersweet) opportunities to sell their company.

There are a countless number of books on starting up, running, and growing successful businesses. However, most of the material available on M&A comprises glorified media stories, and not much quality content has been published on this critical milestone of a startup's exit (pardon the oxymoron). There certainly wasn't anything like this when I was deliberating over my exit option.

I have bootstrapped or self-funded my entrepreneurial pursuits, and I have been in the fortuitous position of not having to raise capital for most of my past companies. If I had, however—Alejandro's book *The Art of Startup Fundraising* would have been my trusted guide.

With this new book, *Selling Your Startup*, Alejandro makes a great contribution to the startup community by addressing the less commonly covered subject of navigating the other end of the startup lifecycle intelligently. Understanding this process can enable you to meaningfully harvest years of hard work.

Whether you are a later stage startup receiving inbound offers or are encountering tough times and contemplating a distress sale, this book will help you build your business with the end in mind. It will help you master the art of the exit. If you foresee one in the near term, then this book will serve as your field guide.

It will walk you through strategies, preparation, paperwork, and processes. It will help you with a decision framework for your next chapter after. After monumental sacrifices, it is a travesty to see founders and teams end up with unfair outcomes during M&A processes. If you want your mission, team, and consumers to continue to flourish beyond an exit, and maximize the outcome for everyone in a win-win manner, then it's time to turn to the next page . . .

—Bhavin Turakhia
Founder
Zeta, Flock, Radix, CodeChef, Directi

SELLING YOUR STARTUP

1

Seeding What Would Grow into Panthera Advisors

I first dipped my toes into the acquisition world while running my previous company, Onevest, which was backed by 14 different venture capital firms.

Building Onevest was a wild ride—full of terrible lows and exceptionally steep highs—but it became one of the largest communities of entrepreneurs, supporting over 500,000 founders in 234 countries.

Onevest and its portfolio of companies provided services such as cofounder matching, accelerator programs, a vibrant Q&A discussion board, key workshops on everything related to building and scaling businesses, and a platform where investors could meet and invest in startups.

It was a dynamic and deeply loyal community.

Accelerated Growth through Acquisitions

On the journey of building and scaling Onevest, part of its growth was organic, which we absolutely lucked out on, but the other part of its growth was attained through acquiring major competitors in the space.

In total, we acquired three of our direct competitors, which was bold and certainly risky, but it turned out to be a strategic move in the end. Two of those transactions, CoFoundersLab and Founder-Dating, were purchased in the millions of dollars and were a bit complex, given all the stakeholders who had a hand in the pot.

In one of those deals, we inherited investors who were not very sophisticated in these sorts of deals. A ton of back-and-forth negotiating ultimately shot the billable lawyer hours through the roof.

As newbie investors, they would either get stuck on standard terms or they would request things different from what was generally accepted in the market. That proved to be a painful but valuable lesson I will never forget. This specific experience is the reason I typically warn entrepreneurs to stay clear of non-sophisticated investors.

These kinds of investors can literally blow up a good deal, or at least significantly complicate things. Believe me, it can be frustrating and complete nonsense when you experience it firsthand. It's almost as if someone is throwing stones at their own glass house—but what can you do?

Yet those specific deals each came with important lessons that really helped me to understand how startup acquisitions work from an operator's perspective.

Acquisitions, to my surprise, were one hundred times harder than rounds of financing. And there's dealing with all types of emotions and egos, so mastering psychology is key.

Inbound Interest and a Path Forward

About eight years into building the business, Onevest started to receive inbound interest from companies that were drawn to our distribution capabilities, data, subscription structure, and access to the venture world.

The offers to buy the company couldn't have come at a better time. I had spent nearly a decade building Onevest with my wife, Tanya Prive, and at that time, she was pregnant with our second and third child (yes, identical twins!). But we soon found out the pregnancy held other surprises for us.

At six months, Tanya was diagnosed with twin-to-twin transfusion syndrome, a rare condition affecting the placenta in identical twin pregnancies where blood is transfused disproportionately from one twin (donor) to the other (recipient), causing the donor to have decreased blood volume and the recipient to be overloaded with blood, which often results in the death of one or both babies. With that diagnosis, Tanya was rushed into the hospital for an emergency C-section.

Our twin daughters were born at 28 weeks gestation, weighing in at 2.4 pounds and 1.7 pounds, respectively, which catapulted us into weeks, and then months, where our baby girls fought for their lives in the hospital. After 129 and 180 days, respectively, at the neonatal intensive care unit (NICU) at Mount Sinai in New York City's Upper East Side, they were finally discharged and able to come home. Our lives had changed, and I knew that stepping back from the daily grind was the right thing to do for myself and Tanya.

Before our girls came home, our four-month-old daughter, Alya, had to undergo heart surgery. As she was wheeled into the operating room, I was preparing the agenda for a board meeting on the four acquisition offers the company had received. I wanted to be near my daughter that day, but the offers left us no choice.

One of the acquisition offers had a 24-hour expiration date. It was December 19 and the members on our board were about to check out for their holiday vacations. It was literally the only time we could get everyone together.

I was a wreck thinking about all the things that could potentially go wrong with Alya's surgery, but I had to sidebar my thoughts to get our board aligned. We unanimously agreed that pursuing an acquisition was in the best interest of our stakeholders. But how did we get to these four acquisition offers in the first place? It all began with me finding Mike Seversen.

Choosing My Wingman

I instinctively knew it wasn't wise for me to tread the transaction path alone, so I began searching for a master banker who would help me navigate any merger and acquisition (M&A) landmines and optimize my chances at a successful exit. To have the best outcome, the deal needed to be viewed not solely as a financial acquisition (all based on revenues and EBITDA) but more as a strategic acquisition.

But in meeting after meeting, I was greeted by more or less the same person: a suit-and-tie Wall Street guy with little to no operating experience. After speaking with tons of potential M&A advisors, I was getting desperate. I knew the kind of person I needed to make the deal a success, and I felt as though I was looking for a needle in a haystack.

Finally, after endless research and asking around, I had a major breakthrough. I connected with Mike Seversen. He was in every sense of the word a true rock star. Sure, he had all the bells and whistles you would expect: Stanford undergrad, MBA Harvard graduate, and a 26-year career in the mergers and acquisitions space, but that wasn't what sold me.

Mike had a rare, heightened emotional intelligence, as well as the operational experience from running his own entrepreneurial ventures. I knew that if anyone could pull off this transaction, it was going to be Mike working with me as a team. I was strong on the business development side and relationship building, and Mike was a wizard of operations, numbers, and creative strategies. He was also keenly skilled in navigating big egos.

Once Mike and I were on the same page, we presented the plan to the board. As soon as the plan received board approval, we immediately got to work.

Our M&A Journey

We ended up with four letters of interest (LOIs) to buy our company. LOIs are the formal way acquirers tell you they are interested in buying your company and at what price, pending a due diligence process. (I'll explain these in more detail later in the book.)

So how did we generate these letters of interest?

First, we went ahead and prepared a list of all the companies we thought could show potential interest in acquiring Onevest. (We're talking here about a list with 300 leads.) We tried to cover every strategic angle we could think of that could trigger interest.

We wanted to target CEOs as opposed to your typical head of corporate development, who usually leads this type of initiative, because the path to a yes is far less risky when a deal comes through the CEO. We knew that if we penetrated the company via the CEO and were handed over to the corporate development team, the team wouldn't hesitate to report back to the CEO if it saw a good fit.

Once we populated our target list with outreach data, we went ahead and reached out to all of the CEOs. In parallel to reaching out to potential acquirers, we also put in motion the formal discussions with the firms that had already expressed direct interest in doing something strategic, which typically means an acquisition.

In essence, this ended up being a four- to six-month process from the start to narrowing down the seriously interested parties.

Out of the 300 leads, we had active conversations with at least 60 of them via phone calls and in-person meetings. From there, we had 25 companies that requested access to the acquisition memorandum (which is the document that lays out the story of your company and what's possible).

Ultimately, it was this process that led us to receive the four letters of interest. In partnership with our board, we ended up taking the LOI that we thought had the best terms and offered the greatest level of alignment with the acquiring management team.

From there, we went into due diligence for three months following the signing of the LOI, and we ultimately closed the deal, which was worth millions. But I can't tell you how many times the transaction nearly blew up.

When all was said and done on the due diligence side, we signed the legal paperwork, got approval from the shareholders, and made the announcement to the world.

Mike and I saw the entire process like a tennis match. He would volley the ball to me when I had to talk about vision or product, and I would volley the ball back to him when terms or negotiations came up.

It was good to remove myself from the difficult conversations about numbers, as well as important clauses in the agreement. This way, when things got tangled up, I could grab the phone and call the CEO directly to keep pushing things forward, sort of like good cop, bad cop.

One thing I knew for sure was that during this stressful process, Mike and I had each other's backs. From day one, we had implicit trust in each other, which I know was a foundational pillar of our success.

Funnily enough, similar to the feeling I had when I met my wife—a feeling of instant connection—I knew Mike was my other half in business. From that day forward, we never looked back.

Launching Panthera Advisors

After the transaction closed and we completed the transition period with Onevest, I called Mike and enrolled him into going into business with me.

I saw two things clearly. For one thing, Mike and I formed a very strong team. He had what I didn't have, and vice versa. But more critically, there was a clear gap in the market. No firm or expert owned the startup acquisition space.

In fact, when I was doing research trying to understand acquisitions for startups, it was like hearing the sound of crickets. Very little information was available to guide founders through this challenging and often complex journey. And I knew that if I had this problem, millions of others did, too.

Luckily, I was thrilled to find out that Mike was equally excited by the idea. As a result, Panthera Advisors was born, as well as the beginning of our journey as partners.

In our first two years, we represented clients in hundreds of transactions globally. Currently, 60 percent of our clients are in the US, and 40 percent of our clients are literally from every single part of the world.

When we get involved with clients, we become an extension of their team. We typically work with the CEO and management for four to six weeks preparing the strategy, the pitchbook with the financials, and the list of targets.

Once these are nailed down, we then go to market, and we're with the client in the trenches every step of the way—during meetings, calls, negotiations, and anything else that arises—until the deal closes.

My Unwavering Commitment to Entrepreneurs

As with Onevest, Panthera Advisors, hundreds of articles, YouTube videos, the *DealMakers* podcast, and *The Art of Startup Fundraising*, this book is the latest addition in my journey to empower entrepreneurs.

Ultimately, the intention of this book is to cover the startup acquisition information gap.

Getting your company acquired is an art. It is also different from fundraising. That's because in fundraising, you need to have everything figured out. With acquisitions, you need to have things *unfigured* out. Essentially, it's not your idea—the idea belongs to whoever is acquiring your business.

This book will equip and guide you through every step of the acquisition process so that you can optimize your chances of exiting your business and getting the best possible deal.

Let's get started!

2

Getting Your Company Acquired

Do you have dreams of getting your company acquired for nine figures, ten figures, or more? Are you already fielding inbound interest in buying your company? Are you trying to stay ahead of the next step in your startup's life cycle? Or maybe you need to run a better process after a failed M&A deal.

Whatever the reason you picked up this book, no worries—you're covered.

Some founders and other key team members get involved with a startup specifically with the hope of quickly cashing out for a record-setting amount. Others swear they will never, ever sell their company, but one day discover that a merger or acquisition is actually the best path for fully realizing and maximizing their mission and vision. In some cases, if your startup is doing well, you will receive inbound offers out of the blue, and much earlier than expected.

In all of these scenarios, this book will help you understand the process, optimize the outcome, and survive the mental marathon.

M&A Is Harder Than Fundraising

Kudos if you've already read the prequel to this book, *The Art of Startup Fundraising*, and have subsequently raised a round of funding, or a few.

Whether you raised equity, used debt financing, or just bootstrapped your venture all the way up to this point, you've already gone through a significant learning curve. You've evolved as an entrepreneur, and you have probably learned much more than you thought you would. You've also learned how to get to market, find product market fit, hire and manage people, and much more.

Acquisitions can be fantastic. In many cases, they can be the best outcome for everyone involved. They can be good for you and your family, your cofounders, your team, your investors, and even your customers. They can be game-changing for so many people. In fact, some hyper-successful serial entrepreneurs will continue launching startups to create ongoing positive outcomes.

But even if you like challenges and learning new things, mergers and acquisitions are not easy.

In many ways, they are like fundraising. There are several crossovers in terms and terminology, tasks, and the materials you'll need. But there are also new concepts, factors—and paperwork—to master.

Mergers and acquisitions will be harder in terms of these factors:

- Time invested throughout every stage of the process
- The crazy hours and schedule needed to get the deal closed
- The mental anxiety and stress level
- How much scrutiny your company is under during due diligence
- Juggling keeping your business on track and managing the deal

The good news is that you don't have to do it again if you don't like it. But like fundraising and working through all of the other quirks of launching a startup, some people end up loving the art of the deal so much that they want to start, scale, and sell businesses over and over again. Just prepare yourself, because it will be challenging.

The Acquisition Process

A great acquisition is a combination of art, science, and execution. The first step to pulling off an acquisition is learning the parts of the process. Figure 2.1 gives you a great 30,000 foot view of what it looks like.

These broad phases of the business acquisition process encompass a lot of details and specifics that we will explore across the entire book:

- **Chapter 2, Getting Your Company Acquired.** To successfully close a deal, facilitate an efficient process, and end up happy with the outcome, you need to learn what potential acquirers are looking for and the pitfalls that await.
- **Chapter 3, The Role of Investment Bankers.** Investment bankers can provide a lot of value and advice, and they're a great asset in helping you set up good cop, bad cop roles.

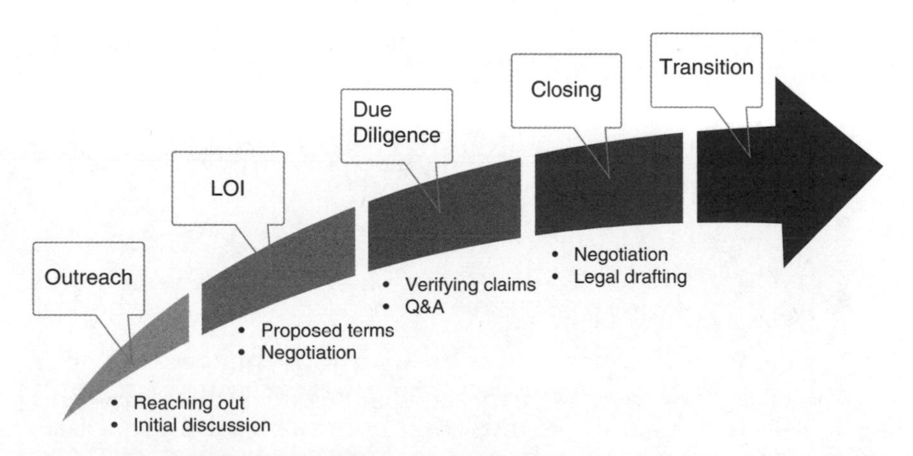

Figure 2.1 Business Acquisitions Process

- **Chapter 4, How to Plan Ahead.** Know why you want to sell, and understand why and how making yourself expendable is important.
- **Chapter 5, Preparing the Company's Pitch Book.** Your pitchbook is where you clarify your uniqueness and value proposition, transition plans, marketing plan, and more. This is where you bring together a proven template for success with the art of presenting the acquisition opportunity for the optimal outcome.
- **Chapter 6, Putting Your Finances in Order.** Everything needs to be properly organized and presented to show off the best picture. Your accounting needs to be polished, you need to have fresh and accurate research at hand, and you need to have the right metrics ready for your presentation.
- **Chapter 7, Understanding Your Valuation.** Make sure you understand the common methods of valuation, where valuation puts your business, and what you can do to strike the best balance of valuation and terms.
- **Chapter 8, Building the Target List.** Find out who the ideal and most likely acquirers of your business are. Filter them and make a short list of your preferences.
- **Chapter 9, The Communication Process with Buyers.** Get to know the paths of connecting with those on your short list, how to make the choice seem obvious to them, and take the conversation through to the next phase.
- **Chapter 10, Preparing for a Successful First Meeting.** Understand your buyer and their concerns, establish the agenda, and follow up.
- **Chapter 11, Getting to a Letter of Intent (LOI).** Learn all the aspects and details of what should be in the LOI and what shouldn't be included.
- **Chapter 12, Communication with Stakeholders.** There is plenty going on that can derail your deal. The last things you

need are internal issues or pushback. Be sure everyone on your side is fully bought in to this move.

- **Chapter 13, Negotiating the Price Tag.** Get ready to negotiate and renegotiate. Know where you can give, where you can't, and how to play the game well.
- **Chapter 14, The Due Diligence Stage.** It's not a done deal until you survive the due diligence phase.
- **Chapter 15, The Purchase Agreement.** Get familiar with purchase agreements, what all of the clauses and terms mean, and who you should deal with.
- **Chapter 16, Strategic versus Financial Acquisitions.** Understand the different types of acquisitions, organizations, buyers, and what matters to them.
- **Chapter 17, Ways to Kill a Deal.** By knowing the many ways the deal can go wrong, you're better situated to handle problems that arise.
- **Chapter 18, Legal Considerations.** There is a lot more to legal considerations than just the contracts and warranties. Regulations, due diligence, working capital, escrow, stockholder approval, liens, and more all come into play.
- **Chapter 19, Closing the Deal.** This is the fun part—actually signing the deal and putting the money in the bank.
- **Chapter 20, Transitioning to a New Phase.** You may stay on with your new company for a while, or you may be ready to accelerate forward into the next venture after an extended, well-earned vacation. Be sure you are thinking ahead.
- **Chapter 21, The Emotional Roller Coaster During Acquisitions.** Acquisitions can bring a whole new set and level of emotions—not just the anxiety of getting the deal done (or not), but also the feelings that come with parting with your startup baby and putting it into someone else's hands—and then figuring out how you'll handle your future plans.

Media versus Your Business: What You See in the Press versus Reality

Just as with fundraising, there can be a big difference between the average merger and acquisition and the sensational headlines you see in the media.

After interviewing hundreds of real-world entrepreneurs on the *DealMakers* podcast—entrepreneurs who have raised amazing money and exited their companies for the grandest outcomes—I've gained and shared the inside scoop on many big deals.

There are certainly startups that have attracted amazing inbound offers in just a year or two since launching. Some have been incredibly fortunate to have found highly competent and efficient acquirers who have run smooth and fast processes. More than a few have sold their companies for billions of dollars.

Others appear to be "overnight successes" after 10 years or more of hard work. Some end up exiting their companies in less-than-ideal circumstances and for much less than expected.

Sometimes board members sabotage the ideal moments to sell for the most dollars. Although exits can happen in only a few weeks, they can often take a year to complete—a long period of extra hustle and stress, which few people talk about.

And although most founders strive for an exit that creates a great future for their startup baby, customers, product, and team, it isn't always as glamorous and profitable as expected. Companies that choose the IPO route often find things go downhill fast in the 12 months after going public. Reverse mergers to take back and revive a company aren't all that uncommon.

If things haven't been structured well for you up to this point, it can lead to huge shortfalls. Did you know that you can sell your company for $1 billion and end up walking away with almost nothing? Due to earnings multiples, seniority, and liquidation preferences, companies appearing to have a lot of equity can leave founders and employees with very little stock at the closing.

When the startup Get Satisfaction sold for $50 million, the founder said he didn't get a penny. The startup Good Technology was valued at $1.1 billion. When the company sold, some employees paid six figures in taxes on their supposed equity, then saw the values of their shares fall from $4.32 to just $0.44.

Even in some of the best scenarios, vesting and resting clauses may mean that you only get half of the announced sale price if you can't stick out the next few years working for your acquirer and hitting the high goals they have set.

The point is, unless you are very careful in structuring equity and legal agreements during the journey, and you understand what they mean in a given exit, those big headlines may not make you feel that good in reality. Sure, the gold star for your résumé might make starting a new venture and raising new money easier, but you should ensure you are getting paid well for all of the sacrifice and work you are putting in.

I often share with entrepreneurs the importance of looking after the founder exit as opposed to just thinking about the business exit. Founders should always keep an eye on the ball. It is all about finding an outcome that justifies all the sweat and tears shed over the course of time.

Acquirer Expectations

What is it that potential buyers want?

Unless you understand what acquirers want, you can't build and position your company to attract them and the best offers. The more intimately familiar you are with these factors, the better you can curate this opportunity for them, and the more power you'll have in negotiations.

This isn't just about understanding their motivations—it's also about what they expect of a target company and its leaders throughout the process, from first talks to the closing table and beyond.

The Process

It is easy to craft a great pitch and sales effort that promises the world. Any used car salesperson, door-to-door vacuum salesperson, or infomercial can do that, though it won't get you far unless you can back it up with facts. Buyers will investigate. They have the responsibility to their own shareholders to make sure that everything adds up.

Accounting

Your accounting needs to be clean. Acquirers may well expect you to be missing out on some key tax savings and potential profits. They may expect to find some issues that give them power to renegotiate better pricing and terms in their favor. The cleaner and more organized you are, the less likely you'll have to deal with these problems. Much of this can also apply to your legal, contracts, debts, and intellectual property (IP).

Investment of Time

Acquirers are going to invest hundreds of labor hours and make a big investment in time and planning to go through this process. They are going to expect you to be willing to do the same and hustle to get the deal done.

It's like if you are trying to buy a house and you are locked up in the contract, but the seller delays handing over documents to the mortgage company and stalls the deal. You wouldn't be happy either. Be prepared to dedicate the time and resources to an intensive and demanding process.

Sharing Risk

Any intelligent acquirer and the teams of experts are going to want you to share in the risk they are taking on. They are risking money, time, and their reputation. There can be long-term risks of the deal not working out that no one will be aware of until a merger plays out. Expect them to want to structure the deal to share this risk between your company and theirs.

A Commitment to Making the Most of the Company

Just because you are going to be consumed with trying to make this deal for the next few months—and may be passing the reins onto someone else—that doesn't mean you can start slacking on the core of your business. You are going to have to keep up the same performance during the process to be able to close on the initial terms. That's true of your growth rate, reputation, revenues, and profitability.

Buyers also want to see that you are setting them up to continue succeeding after the sale. This is why founders will often have noncompete clauses and will be asked to stay on to keep things working for several years after the sale. In most cases, they don't want you to dump a company on their books that is about to fall apart.

Make Them Look Good

All people on the other side of the table want to look good. They want to look good to the people to whom they report. Those people may be team leads, executives, the board of directors, investors, shareholders, and even the public. Be sure you are positioning in a way that helps them achieve that.

We'll dig deeper into some of the motivations for strategic and financial acquisitions later in this book, but here is a quick list of some of the most common:

- Acquiring data
- Acquiring revenues
- Expanding market share

- Maintaining and accelerating their growth
- Securing IP
- Acquihires to bring in better talent
- Blocking their competition
- Adding new verticals and products efficiently
- Getting a good financial deal

Why Most Acquisitions Fail

According to CB Insights, 70 percent of startups fail after their first financing round; 97 percent of some categories, such as hardware startups, eventually die or become zombies.

If you've made it this far, you've already beaten many of the odds. Yet, 60 percent or more of all acquisitions fail, too. Some put the number as high as 90 percent, so you are not out of the woods yet.

The following sections examine some of the top reasons that these M&A deals fail during the process or within the next couple of years after a sale.

That Was the Plan

In some cases, the talks aren't designed to lead to a closing. They might just want to take a peek under the hood of your company to see what makes it run. They may just want to tie you up in the process. In other situations, it may be cheaper to buy you as a way to take you out of the equation as a competitor. They may just buy you to shut you down.

It Wasn't What They Expected

After digging into the data and facts during due diligence, the prospect of buying your company may not offer what they hoped to find, or it didn't live up to the hype. There can be all types of issues with equity structures, debt, contracts, and other legal problems. Most founders are completely oblivious to these as well.

Incompetence

Not many companies and entrepreneurs have a lot of experience with M&A. They may not have an organized acquisition or onboarding process. It could be their first time. Even with larger companies, new hires can potentially throw a wrench in things.

Some say that even the largest tech companies that have completed large numbers of acquisitions aren't always competent at integrating and operating new acquisitions. They do some things really well at scale, but they may not always be great at getting the most out of a new small startup. This can be made more difficult, because those you deal with in the acquisition process may just be dumping your company in someone else's lap after the closing. They may not have the same vision, priorities, or appreciation for it.

Integration

Integration is probably the number one reason that acquisitions fail to work out well after the fact. You are marrying two opposites with completely different cultures—two companies that often have completely different values, priorities, mindsets, and systems of operating. That's challenging.

Changing Markets and Circumstances

Things can change rapidly in the months it can take to close a deal. Just look at how quickly the COVID-19 pandemic altered businesses and the economy.

Factors like this can completely change the valuation and appeal for certain companies, as well as confidence and urgency in completing deals. But on the bright side, changes can also dramatically work in your favor, too.

Knowing these pitfalls will greatly help your company ace the M&A process and avoid massive amounts of wasted time and energy, while perhaps positioning the deal for an even stronger outcome.

3

The Role of Investment Bankers

WHAT ROLE DO INVESTMENT BANKERS play in M&A?

Unless you went to school to study to become an investment banker, or you did a stint in investment banking as an intern or after college, you may have had little experience with them thus far. Sooner or later, you'll probably be pitched by one if you are doing well.

So, how do investment bankers play into M&A? When should you bring them into the deal? How do you pick one, and how much do they cost?

What Is an Investment Banker?

Investment bankers can do a lot of things in finance. They can act as financial advisors, prepare prospectuses, aid in US Securities and Exchange Commission (SEC) paperwork when filing for an IPO, and advise acquirers on the best ways to structure purchases of other companies, helping them find the money to do so.

When it comes to the sell side of M&A, investment bankers can help you value your company, advise you on terms and deal structures, negotiate on your behalf, and help pitch and sell your business to other companies.

In essence, an investment banker is like an agent or broker who matches buyers and sellers and financiers for corporations.

Good Cop, Bad Cop

Which cop is going to show up at your startup?

Like all salespeople, investment bankers often play good cop, bad cop. It often depends on their style and what they've been taught. Either way, their advice may not be wrong, but it may not always be offered in a style you are used to or receptive to.

They want to get the deal done. That's how they get paid. Sometimes they may try to accomplish this by trying to inspire you about what is possible with an exit. In other cases, they may try to pressure you into a deal. The pressure may appear when it comes to negotiating terms and deal structures. Of course, you don't want to be selling yourself short.

You also don't want to fall into the trap of overvaluing your company, or accepting terms you shouldn't, under the pressure of closing. Lean on your other trusted advisors for their experienced opinions, for backup when you are being hustled, or when you need to ensure (or really need to hear) that there is truth to what the investment banker is telling you.

There is another good cop, bad cop scenario to consider. Hiring an investment banker can also give you the ability to play good cop, bad cop with potential acquirers. It is an effective negotiation and management technique.

An investment banker acting as an agent and buffer between you and the other side can have a lot of advantages. It helps you negotiate better deals that really work in your favor and avoid giving in to asks that you'll deeply regret later on.

This is something we see when working with clients at Panthera Advisors. We essentially take the lead on uncomfortable discussions about terms that require tense negotiations. This way, the client is always on the positive side of building the relationship.

Why Bankers Add Value

In addition to running interference in the middle of both parties and negotiations, and all of the time and stress this can save you, there are a variety of ways that bankers can bring value to the table.

They Are Experts at Pitching

Maybe you've become pretty good at pitching for fundraising by this point, though pitching for M&A is obviously different in a variety of ways.

Experienced bankers already have a handle on the art of the deal—at least the real dealmakers (not just your interns and entry-level analysts and associates at big firms). They've done this at least a dozen times already, and they should know what to say. They should also know the pitfalls you may be overlooking.

Established firms have teams to work on preparing M&A pitch-books, and this may help you save time and energy so that you can spend more of your time focusing on running the business rather than being distracted.

They Can Run Valuations

Bankers are also experts at running valuations. They do it every day. Whether you want to use them to run the whole process, from testing the waters of the market to closing, or you and your board need a third-party valuation opinion for liability purposes, or you simply want them to check interest in additional bids after receiving an inbound offer, they can help.

They See the Maximum Potential Value of Your Startup

Investment bankers have a whole different perspective on company value. They can see a lot of the strategic value you may otherwise be leaving on the table.

They have a big picture view of the M&A horizon. They understand what's happening in the market in ways you may not see or that haven't been reported in the media yet. At the least, it's hearing that potential version of a sale and what's possible. (Just remember their motivations.)

They Handle the Paperwork

They can handle a lot of the paperwork. You should know your way around LOIs, purchase agreements, and so on. You want to be educated, and you want to know what to look for in the fine print and not be taken for being a complete novice.

Though the paperwork is intensive, it is important. Every clause can be impactful. Letting a pro take care of it for you can be more efficient and may help you avoid serious mistakes—at least with your first rodeo.

They Know the Players

If they've been in the business for a while, bankers know the other players in the field. They know which companies may be looking to acquire what types of startups, who is really buying, the good buyers versus the bad ones, and so on.

They should also have connections to the right departments and decision-makers so they can get you through to some of your target buyers much faster than starting cold.

They Know How to Stretch to Help Get Deals Done

Bankers are also deep into corporate finance, so they know how to help buyers stretch to make acquisitions. They can help them raise capital and find loans to buy people out if they need it.

Getting the Right Advice

If you've made it this far, you already know the power of great advice. So how do you continue to get great advice through the M&A transaction? How do you pick the right investment banker for your deal?

Choosing the right banker is important. So is balancing their advice with input from your existing trusted advisors and your gut instincts.

Trusted Referrals

This is not a service you want to play Yellow Pages roulette with or rely on Siri for. Look to your investors, advisors, and other founders who've recently exited for recommendations of trustworthy and capable investment bankers.

Long-Term Experience

Just as your startup has no doubt involved years of trial and error and iterating, so does investment banking and M&A. You don't want to be one of the first guinea pigs for someone who is new to this role.

It can take years to encounter and master the nuances and gotchas in selling companies. Find someone who has been around long enough to be truly knowledgeable.

Investment bankers who have been involved in numerous transactions have probably developed not only the expertise but also the pattern recognition for how to handle certain situations they may have experienced in the past.

That pattern recognition ultimately optimizes your potential outcome.

Domain Experience

Beyond the general sell-side M&A experience, you want a banker who has experience specific to your space and type of business—someone who knows health care or SaaS or marketplaces, or whatever your angle is.

They'll have experience dealing with the complications, and they'll know the nooks where value is hiding. They will have a strong Rolodex of contacts that are on your target buyer's list.

In addition, don't just look at company brand names. It is the individual you will be working with that matters most. That person should be an expert in the size of transaction you are hoping for. This is also important for ensuring fee scales align.

Not Just What You Want to Hear

You don't want to choose the banker who only tells you what you want to hear, makes it sound easier, or who promises you can sell for the highest, top-line price. That's a huge red flag for disaster later. In truth, you don't even have to really like your banker.

You need someone who will be straight with you, who will prepare you well for what's ahead, and someone who will be honest, even if that person knows you won't like it.

Breaking Down the Fees

How much do investment bankers cost? What are their fees? Is it worth using them?

Some say they are too expensive. Others find they are a bargain and wouldn't consider ever taking the DIY route. There may be some scenarios in which you already have a strong M&A team or have a substantial head start in strategizing and preparing for an exit.

In other cases, taking the do-it-yourself approach to selling a large company is like someone without the right education or experience trying to put on his or her own legal defense in a life-or-death situation, or a non-physician hospital owner jumping in to perform open heart surgery. You can imagine the consequences and lawsuits.

Investment bankers can charge a variety of types of fees, as shown in figure 3.1.

The following sections examine these fees in more detail.

Retainers and Up-Front Fees

Just like any good attorney, marketing agency, or consultant, you can expect a good banker to ask for a retainer. This ensures you are serious and ensures the banker gets paid for his or her time.

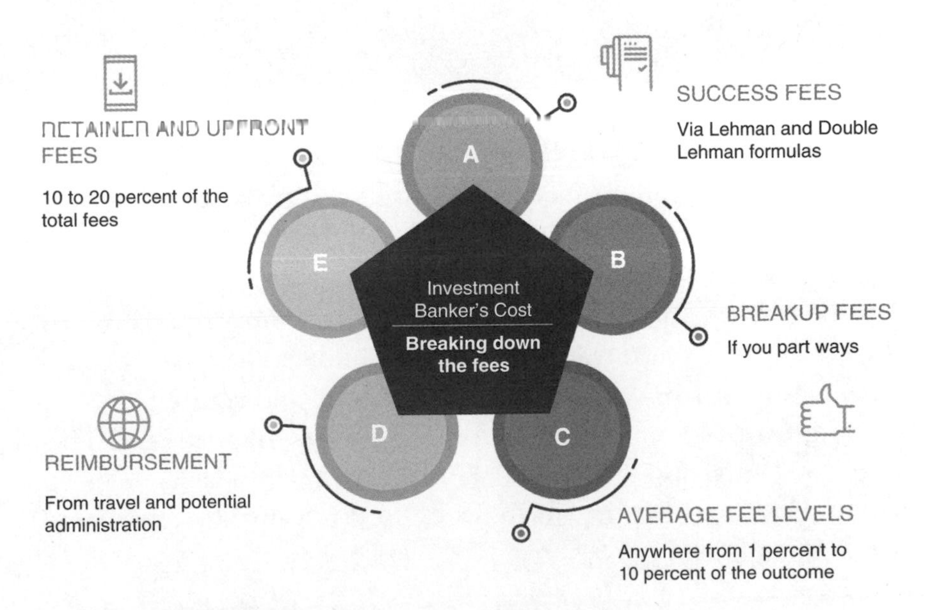

Figure 3.1 Banker Fees

Retainers may represent anywhere from 10 percent to almost 20 percent of total fees. There should be a written agreement ahead of time stating how much monthly retainer fees can scale to, and the maximum caps for the total period of this process. Expect to put up a minimum of $5,000 to $15,000 as an initial monthly retainer.

On larger deals, retainers can be at least $100,000. Larger firms have more overhead and don't need to beg for deals. They often filter by which deals are going to be the most profitable or notable to engage in. Expect equally notable retainers.

Reimbursement

In addition to covering their hourly work on the deal, you can expect to cover or reimburse investment banking companies for their out-of-pocket expenses associated with working your deal. This may include travel, hotels, and so on. Otherwise, they can end up spending a lot of money out-of-pocket up-front, without any guarantee of you coming through on closing the deal and recouping their hard costs.

Success Fees

Success fees are really like commissions. They are paid on the successful sale of your business and completed closing.

This is one of the best ways to ensure alignment. You only pay these fees when the deal is done and your company gets paid. Just always be sure to read the fine print and understand what the real distributions are for your investors, your team, and yourself.

There are several structures for success fees, like flat fees. This may especially apply on smaller, more work-intensive deals in which bankers want to make sure they cover their costs and needed margins.

Similarly, there can also be set percentages (for example, 10 percent). In this case, no matter how much or little your company is sold for, you pay the same percentage success fee.

There are also scaled percentage fees. Most common is the Lehman and Double Lehman.

The Double Lehman calls for the following fee structure:

- 10 percent on the first $1 million
- 8 percent on the second $1 million
- 6 percent on the third $1 million
- 4 percent on the fourth $1 million
- 2 percent on any additional proceeds

The regular Lehman scale is only half of these percentages.

There are also reverse-scaled percentage fees. So in contrast to the Lehman scale, business brokers or investment banking firms will earn an increasing percentage the more they sell your company for.

This may provide the most alignment and motivation for them to get you the highest price. How much you actually net and love the deal will still depend on the terms.

Keep in mind that on fundraising, anyone receiving a commission that is subject to the outcome of the transaction is required to be registered as a broker dealer with FINRA in order to comply with the rules of the SEC.

If you use a non-registered broker to facilitate a fundraise, and you pay that person a success fee, then in the event the company doesn't perform as investors expected, the company can literally sue you to get its money back for having used someone without the proper broker-dealer license.

However, in acquisitions, there is no need to be licensed as a broker-dealer. The SEC issued a no-action letter in 2014 that allowed people to be entitled to success fees without the need for registration.

Breakup Fees

Your agreement may also include breakup fees. Think of these as cancellation fees.

Breakup fees may be incurred if you change your mind, or back out of the deal and the banker has incurred costs, if you prove to be too difficult, or you haven't been transparent in representing what you have or in dealing with the potential buyers the banker has brought you.

Know how much the breakup fee is, because you'll have to pay it if you choose to walk away, if you turn down an offer that matches your ask, or you just choose to raise another round of financing or go public instead.

Average Fee Levels

Trends and fees can vary over time. As a very rough guide to fees, here's what you can expect to pay based on the acquisition price:

- $0 to $10 million: 10 percent
- $10 million to $100 million: 3 percent to 10 percent
- $100 million to $1 billion+: 1 percent to 2 percent

4

How to Plan Ahead

ALTHOUGH YOU'VE ALREADY LEARNED THAT entrepreneurship requires a lot of flexibility and long-range planning, you also know the pains associated with failing to plan and looking far enough into the future.

You may never plan to sell your company. Or maybe you've had your eyes set on an IPO. Yet, if you build a great company, then it's likely an M&A deal will come looking for you. It may prove to be the best exit for many reasons.

If you build your business in a way that sets it up for an attractive acquisition, you'll also be building a strong company that will have great long-term potential as a private business or that is poised for an IPO or further fundraising. Having a merger or acquisition as a possible exit strategy will give you the most flexibility and strength for several possible outcomes.

Most startups don't think far enough ahead to position themselves for an M&A exit. When it does become an option (or a necessity), that lack of planning is going to take a big bite out of the price tag. Inadequate planning means inferior terms in a sale. The whole process will be a whole lot more intensive and stressful.

Think of it like returning a leased Maserati. If you ensured proper maintenance, kept it in pristine condition, washed it, did oil changes on schedule, put in the right gas, avoided any damage, and didn't exceed your miles, then on returning it, the dealership would be more than happy to upgrade you to something even better. Perhaps with just a signature, you could be in and out of the dealer in an hour.

However, if you let your teenagers use that Maserati as their first car, and they decide to use it like an old 4×4 off-road center-of-the-party Jeep over three long years, you can expect a completely different outcome when you go to the dealer. The dealer is going to ding you for every scratch and dent at several hundred or several thousand dollars a pop, and the bigger issues may cost you a whole lot more. You could get a bill for tens of thousands of dollars just to turn it in and get rid of it. And when the dealer sends that car to auction, it will sell for a tiny fraction of its original value.

Smart startups plan for the exit from the start, even before day one. They craft their company with the end in mind, as well as what their plan B or plan C exit might be.

This can include the way you incorporate the business and where, the legal documents you use, compensation packages offered, who is offered equity, how capital is brought in, how well-rounded the company is, and on down to the software and systems used for daily operations.

If you hope to play and exit at a high level, then it just makes sense to create a company that is ready to do that on its own or that can easily be evaluated and integrated with another company at this level.

It's like landlords who want to grow a portfolio of rental properties and sell them to a big fund for a grand exit. If they haven't kept good accounting records and they don't have records of all the rents they have or haven't collected, the bills on the properties, documentation of improvements made, or copies of leases, a big fund is going to have a hard time making sense of it all.

They are probably just going to walk away—or at best maybe a slumlord will offer a deeply discounted cash price in the worst-case scenario.

Compare that to another landlord with sets of apartment buildings in Brooklyn or Miami who has professional management in place and uses the same terminology and accounting calculations and software as the big fund. It makes a world of difference in the price and speed of the deal and the ability to choose a buyer who will take good care of the legacy, communities, and tenants.

Curate your company well, and the process of selling may only be weeks-long instead of a year. The valuation is going to be much better. There will be far fewer sleepless nights, wrinkles, bald spots, and therapy sessions needed when you are done.

You'll also have a much greater choice of acquirers, and that could make all the difference in how happy you are with the outcome of the venture.

Consider the Reasons Why You Want to Sell

There may be several reasons you eventually decide to sell your business. Some you may plan for. Others will emerge years down the road. Some may create the right timing to sell your business.

Here are just a few of the most common reasons business owners end up selling.

Getting to the Next Level of Scale and Customers

You might get to a point where growth is leveling off and it will take a lot more investment, know-how, and a bigger team to get to the next level. (That may be going national or expanding to international markets.) Expanding may be a big risk and long path and will require a lot more capital.

Merging with another company to combine forces or to leverage its expertise in these markets can be a great move.

Efficient Growth

You have to keep on growing, but you also need to be able to grow efficiently and profitably. Imagine plugging your product or service into Google or the equivalent in your industry. Google can take it to millions or billions of users instantaneously. Some may add it to their catalog, bundle it with theirs to offer more value, or vice versa.

Advancing the Mission

Selling or merging your company may be the best way to continue the mission you set out on. It may be the most effective (or only) way to enable the company's full potential and fully realize your vision.

If you really want to have the maximum impact and create change at scale, then putting your product or service in the hands of someone who is more equipped to do this may be necessary.

The Value Has Peaked

In many cases, the reason companies sell or go public is that they have peaked. There may be room for slow and steady growth in the future, or in the right hands it can be a cash-producing asset to keep in a portfolio—though often, the best growth and value has been reached, and investors want to cash out before things stall or decline.

You Get an Offer Too Good to Refuse

If you are doing everything right, you may attract offers that are just too good to turn down. It may be foolish to turn them away. Or you legally may not have the ability to choose to turn them down on your own. Of course, that doesn't mean you have to take the first offer. You might be surprised how much more you can get by holding out for their second or third offer or by shopping around with that offer in hand.

You Get an Opportunity to Advance Your Learning

If you thrive on a challenge and learning, then rolling your company into another larger one can bring those opportunities. You may not want to work for someone else again for very long, but many founders love the experience of being able to learn what great looks like at the highest levels and to work alongside and learn from those at the very top of the game. It may be just what you need to take your next venture to even greater heights.

Fundraising Challenges

The market can change on you. Surprises in the economy can emerge, and your industry or operations can make it very difficult to raise another round of financing—or, at least, to raise a round on terms that are appealing and make sense. This might be a good time to explore your exit alternatives.

Creating a Great Outcome for Your Team

Those who have experienced what a great exit can do for their team members get excited about replicating that outcome for others, and they want to repeat it.

A successful exit is a great way to reward your team for their belief in you, the sacrifice for the mission, and all the hard work. It can also be game changing for them, their families, and others they touch through their lives and legacy.

Starting, scaling, and selling startups is a fantastic way to keep multiplying that impact.

Personal Reasons

Crises can arise that mean you need to be there for your family. Or you may just be burned out and you crave or need a lifestyle change for your health. Or it could just be an opportunity to cash out and secure the gains you have created.

You may see an opportunity to completely change your finances and stability, where you can go on to do new things from a position of being able to pursue what is important to you, and not just to make money.

Moving On to the Next Thing

Maybe you just need to free yourself up to move on to the next thing. Perhaps you are excited about a new project or problem and just want the freedom to go all-in. You could just be bored, and you crave starting something new from scratch.

In other cases, it becomes clear that the business is going to be capped in potential. It may be a great business, a meaningful one, and a profitable one. It just may never be a multibillion dollar giant. Others sell because the dynamics of the company change. They run into disputes with partners and investors and become unhappy with the direction, values, and culture that has developed. In these scenarios, it can make sense to just move on.

Tying Up Loose Ends

Whatever leads you to sell, you can take several steps to organize and clean up in order to ensure you maximize the exit.

Cleaning Up Legal

Buyers don't like unknowns. When they encounter them, it just makes sense to price in the worst-case scenario, which usually means big discounts off the real situation for the seller. Do as much as you can to close up any potential risks and remove question marks.

This includes cleaning up operating agreements, intellectual property registrations, employment contracts, and contracts with outside vendors, as well as any pending lawsuits or complaints. Make sure everything is organized and up-to-date.

Paying Off the Debt

There is more than one way to structure a sale. Debts and financial liabilities can be viewed and handled differently depending on whether the sale is a stock sale or asset sale and how different assets are treated.

If you started off scrappy and bootstrapping, you may need to pay off any debts that you have personally guaranteed. You don't want those liabilities in someone else's hands.

In addition to looking at debt-to-equity ratios, keep in mind that debts are always a form of risk. Although it may seem logical to just deduct liabilities from assets, it is also worth considering that the buyer may be able to buy some of these assets that are financed much cheaper. They may also be able to finance them cheaper or they may find it better to use excess capital.

Paying off debt can definitely make your business look stronger—providing you don't leave too little working capital and runway, which could bite you if negotiations are drawn out.

The Importance of Making Yourself Expendable

One of the big differences between true hyper-growth startups that are scalable and salable and businesses that remain smaller lifestyle businesses and are more likely to close down than to be acquired or go public is how expendable the founders are. Contrary to what you may have been taught, in an acquisition, being expendable is a good thing.

Why is this so important, and how do you do it?

The Ability to Sell Your Business

Many entrepreneurs have a difficult time delegating and empowering others. They struggle to step back to let other people do their best work and make decisions. They end up building the business all around themselves and making the business rely on them to work.

Not only does that mean this approach doesn't work if you get sick, want to go on vacation, or need to go on leave, it doesn't really make a salable business. You *are* the business. It would make a whole lot more sense for them to simply employ you than to buy your company.

Traditionally, there's something good to be said about buying businesses with good management teams. Yet, when it comes to buying and selling startups, it is better to have a machine that can work just as well in anyone's hands—especially a new team that specializes in taking the business to the next level and phase of its life cycle.

Price

There is clearly a massive difference in the value between an autonomous and scalable company and acquiring a salesperson or technologist who generates revenue, has incorporated him- or herself, and may have built a team of assistants.

Not Being Stuck Staying On for Years

Even if you do pull off a big exit, if you haven't made yourself fully expendable, then your acquirer is going to demand you stay on for several years to run it.

As much as half the price of your acquisition may be reliant on you sticking with the new company, successfully hitting their KPIs, and ensuring the business is integrated. So why not tackle this earlier and get a better price and more freedom in the first place?

How to Make Yourself Expendable

There are a variety of ways to set things up right from the beginning and avoid expendability becoming an issue.

Branding

Be sure you are branding the business in its own right and not just yourself. There may be ongoing benefits of building up your own brand, but it is all about you. If you focus on yourself, there is little differentiation from your personal brand and the company. You are throwing away a lot of equity value and sabotaging a potential sale.

Athletes have their own personal brands, but great teams worth the most money don't rely on any one player's brand. The Lakers and Heat are worth a substantial amount of money. Teams at that level are bought without any guarantee of a certain player being on the court next season. They come and go. Most people don't even know the coaches' or owners' names.

Virgin may be a standalone brand without Richard Branson, but it was really difficult for people to believe Apple could be as good without Steve Jobs. Right now, few may believe Berkshire Hathaway will keep its appeal without Warren Buffett.

Hire Great People

One of the top pieces of advice from successful repeat entrepreneurs is to hire a high-quality executive team as early as possible. Hire from the top down, not the bottom up. Let your department heads run their departments and teams, rather than just recruiting the equivalent of a bunch of assistants, and then trying to insert a new manager over them and between you later.

Set Yourself in the Right Role from the Beginning

Build your company with the end in mind. Build it as you want it to end up, right from the beginning, rather than hoping you can switch it up at some mythical date in the future. That should be at least from the CEO level, if not chairman of the board—someone overseeing things from above, not the lead salesperson or technologist.

Start as the owner and be interchangeable with another owner. You don't want to be a doer in the trenches or the sole superstar.

5

Preparing the Company's Pitchbook

Your company's pitchbook or *acquisition memorandum* is a vital piece of the puzzle for achieving the best possible exit. Like a pitch deck in equity fundraising, a pitchbook is about presenting your business and the opportunity, and selling both.

If you're thinking you've become pretty adept at whipping up pitch decks to raise capital on the fly and so the pitchbook will be a breeze, you should know that creating a pitchbook is a little more in-depth.

You'll have more to present, and the expectations of readers will be much higher. You may not be running ads or putting a for sale sign in your window, but your pitchbook is your chance to make the pitch and present the vision of the outcome of your companies working together to create value.

Packaging the Message

So how do you package all of your pertinent information, the data on your company, *and* deliver a subtle sales pitch?

Aside from more sensitive and in-depth data (which should be uploaded to your deal room in the cloud with revocable access), the best way to convey all of the necessary information is in a slide format, similar to a pitch deck.

Although effective pitch decks have become more condensed and simplified, when you get to the stage of selling your business, your presentation will need to have a lot more meat on the bone.

As a starting point, consider that you now probably have a lot more hard data and information to share versus when you first floated your idea in your deck for your pre-seed round.

Then, you want to consider that the viewers of your pitchbook are also far more focused on facts, data, and numbers than early-stage startup investors riding on the vapor of your vision and optimism.

However, don't overlook the ability to make your offering much more compelling, sticky, and valuable by creating a new vision of what could be for your acquirer. There is still a lot of art of the sale at this juncture. Don't throw away millions by neglecting the opportunity.

What Makes Your Company Unique?

There are millions of companies out there. There are probably at least thousands in your industry. Even in your product and technology and position in the supply chain, there are probably at least dozens, if not hundreds, of potentially qualified companies. So what makes your company unique?

Buyers have options (including just building it themselves), so what is so special about your business that you should be the one they spend so much time and money on?

By now, you should have your unique selling proposition definitively nailed when it comes to your customers and selling your product or service. It's a crucial factor at this point in the life of your company as well. Are you faster, leaner, cheaper, more loved, or more efficient? What is it that your competition can't say about themselves and match you on?

In this context, it is also important to clearly convey what is unique, particularly valuable, and exclusive about your business as a potential acquisition and asset. What are your buyers going to get from acquiring you that they won't get elsewhere? What is that unique thing they can only gain from buying your company over the competition? What is your competitive advantage in this context?

Here are some examples of the aspects that may apply here:

- Your team
- Your trademarked and patented technology
- Your customer base and relationship with them
- Your data
- What you've de-risked
- Your proven ability to work well with their company
- Your track record of success

Nailing the Value Proposition for Potential Acquirers

The value proposition for potential acquirers should be much more than just acquiring your existing assets.

If you are profitable and cash is flowing well, there can be some tentative value in those returns for financial buyers. If your company is a purely asset-based purchase, even if it comes down to income streams and returns, it becomes about discounts. How much less can they buy your assets and company for than it's worth to lock in profit and insulate against risk? If this is your only sales pitch, it is pretty obvious that the whole conversation and post–term sheet negotiations are going to be focused on how they can drive down that price and buy you cheap. That isn't the direction you want to head in.

Even in a fire sale situation, on the doorstep of bankruptcy, you want to maximize the outcome as much as possible.

This is where the real art of deal-making and selling a business comes in.

Eight, nine, or ten figures can be added to the valuation of your company and the deal by really nailing the value proposition.

This is a pain-to-pleasure equation. What pain are they in that they need a painkiller for? What pain are they going to be in that they will need a cure for at any cost, in the near future, if they don't act now?

What pleasure do they seek? How can acquiring your company help them achieve their goals and aspirations—not only in how the stock market is going to react over the next few quarters but also in the grand scheme of things and the long term for their company?

It is also important to keep in mind here that these are still humans you are engaging with. All of them have their own ego, fears, pains, and aspirations. They don't want to mess up in front of their bosses or board. They do want to look smart and be praised for making great moves.

A big part of the pitchbook, maybe 30 percent or more, is forecasting a vision and modeling the fantastic upside potential of this merger or acquisition deal.

Be sure you are laying this out in line with their goals, strategies, and plans, not yours. But be sure to paint a very vivid picture of what the outcome can be, at its best.

Here are some of the key points you may want to make here based on the individual situation:

- How you can save their brand from becoming crusty and irrelevant and help them become hot and respected again
- The competitive advantages you can secure for their company
- The rate of growth, revenues, and profitability you can add for them

Defining Transition Plans for Potential Buyers

Don't be so consumed with making a deal and getting to closing that you overlook post-closing. This is where the real make-or-break is.

Acquirers know this. They also know you may be distracted with the rest of the process. A significant percentage of your payday may actually rely on post-closing performance, integration, and the ability to reach the goals set for the next few years.

It's not just about the money, either. This is where your company can get chopped up and broken into pieces, or folded and discarded, along with your mission and vision.

Showing that you've thought through this next phase in advance will say a lot about you as a leader. They won't see you as an easy target to take advantage of. It also shows that you are serious about making this acquisition a success for them after the sale.

They may well have their own ideas and plans for merging and absorbing your company and its assets and people, and many of these elements can change once the company is handed off to new teams within their organization. However, it is still valuable to take the time to lay out a potential path, or paths, for the next phase.

Much of this may be embodied in a transitional services agreement, which lays out factors such as these:

- The services each party will provide post-closing
- Who will cover the costs of this transition
- What third parties may be involved and who chooses them
- What happens to rights, data, and so on
- The ability to review and audit
- How defaults on this agreement and its provisions will be escalated and the penalties
- Who assumes which liabilities
- Wind-down plans

Do not leave these things to chance. Be sure they are being negotiated early. It is all a part of knowing your real exit from this arrangement before you get into it.

Crafting the Marketing Plan

If you are serious about pulling off an exit and the timing is right, then you can't afford to be too passive. You need to have a marketing budget and a highly talented team of creatives to tell the right story about the right data points and triggers.

A successful campaign always starts with a well-thought-out research strategy and plan. This isn't one of those times when you can afford to just throw things against the wall on a whim and keep iterating and optimizing for the next few years. That time luxury isn't available, and the execution can mean a difference of tens of millions of dollars and a lot more.

This requires a subtle strategy. Not passive, but subtle. You aren't overtly advertising your business for sale.

You are subconsciously planting the idea that they should buy your company, that this is the best time for them to do it. Plant the fear of missing out if they don't hustle and do something about it.

Do this with branding and be in their face, dropping the right clues that this is the best value time to acquire your company, and some type of exit is imminent—if not to them, then one of their competitors. So make sure you include the right contact information if you want to get follow-through. Get them to compete over you.

Start with your research to best reach your target list of acquirers. Where are they? What do they read? When is the best time to get in front of them?

Here are some of the ways you may achieve this:

- Email updates
- Blogs
- Press releases
- Guest appearances on podcasts

- Advertorials
- Social media: LinkedIn, Twitter, and popular industry-specific platforms

Identifying a Powerful Flow and Structure

What does a great pitchbook or acquisition memorandum look like?

Flow and structure are incredibly important. You need to include all of the expected information, and you need to make sure everything is correct. Be sure to leave out all other facts that are just going to bog inquirers down or turn them off at this point.

As with a fundraising pitch deck, just having the right information isn't enough. The information has to flow in the right order. You might have all of the pieces of a puzzle spread out on the floor, but it doesn't make a great picture unless they are put together correctly. Or you can have all the right wiring and all of the right types of switches to wire your office building, but if they are connected by an unlicensed amateur over the weekend, it can be a very dangerous disaster waiting to happen.

An acquisition memorandum can be broken down into three sections:

- **Current status.** What's going on with your company? What is the asset?
- **The problem.** What is the acquirer's problem that you can solve?
- **The solution.** How does a merger or acquisition provide a solution, and how great is it?

If you're using a vertical PDF or printed paper layout, use short paragraphs to break things up. If you are opting for a more modern slide presentation–based layout, you'll be working horizontally, and you'll need to use short statements and bullet points.

Select a background, color scheme, and font that fits your company brand. Use plenty of pictures to keep it interesting for the reader (and charts and diagrams, too, of course).

Acquisition Memorandum Template

This acquisition memorandum template[1] is adapted from the pitchbook template published on my website, along with many other business templates and forms for startups.[2]

There are a number of slides to include in your acquisition memorandum:

- Cover slide
- Disclosures
- Table of contents
- Executive summary
- Market opportunity
- Solution
- Target market
- Competition and advantages
- Market traction
- Financial results and projections
- Executive team
- Technology platform
- Marketing and sales
- Business history
- Reason for the sale
- Buyer qualifications
- Directions for the LOI

The following sections examine these slides more closely.

Cover Slide

Be sure to include your contact information, company name, and brand image. The cover slide is like a movie trailer for your acquirer.

---

[1] https://alejandrocremades.com/aquisition-memorandum-template/

[2] https://alejandrocremades.com/business-templates/

You want this slide to set up expectations so that viewers get an idea of what they are going to review, and you want to illustrate that the movie will be something that they might find interesting. Try to go the extra mile with a powerful design—use visuals that tell what you are doing right away.

Keep in mind that more companies are using horizontal slides for the acquisition memorandum. If you use the vertical format, you want to make sure the headers are the same. With the horizontal format, you want to use more bullets and short statements, whereas with the vertical format, it is better to go with short paragraphs.

Disclosures

Be sure to include the necessary disclosures pages that your M&A attorney will insist on. The disclosures could take up to three slides, but to cover your back, you want to include whatever is necessary.

Table of Contents

Make your acquisition memorandum more easily navigable and show them what you've included. This way, if they want to jump quickly to a section that may be of more interest, they can easily navigate through the document.

Executive Summary

Sum it all up in the executive summary. This can be tailored to each potential acquirer. This is the page that will determine whether they keep reading or not.

Market Opportunity

Allow for two to three slides in this section, as needed. Use graphics and big data points. Include interesting facts and stats they may not yet be aware of. Here you want to talk about timing and why your company is at the right time in history.

Solution

This may be broken down into three to five slides, explaining your business and the solution it is providing.

- What is the product or service?
- How does it work?
- How do you make money?
- What is the business model?

Keep it very simple. Use flowcharts and images.

Target Market

Who is the addressable market? How big is it? How much is it growing?

Competition and Advantages

This may be very similar to your SWOT analysis and competitor slide in your fundraising pitch deck. Make sure you adjust it to be most relevant for the M&A context. Use a graphic.

Market Traction

Allow for two to three pages of financial metrics and KPIs and highlight your growth, milestones, customer acquisition volume, revenues, and so on.

Financial Results and Projections

Display your past three years of historical financial data, followed by your next five years of financial projections for your company as is, and with current plans.

Then, you may display financial models and projections of what could be possible with partnership, merger, or acquisition with the party.

Try to avoid including screenshots from your financial model. Instead, extract that data into beautiful slides showing the information in a way that potential acquirers can digest easily.

Executive Team

Allow one to two slides to present your executive team. Use headshots, titles, names, and a one- or two-sentence bio.

Your team is going to be a critical asset. Make sure you are capturing why you have the right people in the right seats. Talk about prior experiences as well as accomplishments.

Technology Platform

List the technology being used in your stack. Potential buyers will be most interested in the split between how much of the tech is leased from other companies or open-sourced versus the proprietary tech that has tangible value, what you have built, and the IP that you have the rights to sell.

Potential buyers may want to bring in technical advisors for review, so the more you describe the key components, the better.

Marketing and Sales

Use images or bullet points to explain your sales and marketing strategy and channels. What are your methods of customer acquisition?

This may also be an opportunity to show the advantages of merging your companies and the additional efficiencies, value, and profits from making a deal.

Hopefully if you do a good job with this slide, the potential buyers may start to dream about what it could look like if you were under their umbrella. They may also contemplate how your competitive advantage could help catapult some of their other initiatives.

Business History

Include a quick time line of your company history. When did you start? What are the notable milestones you've accomplished?

You could even follow this with a road map of some of the plans you had in place.

Reason for the Sale

Why are you selling or willing to sell your company now? Are you selling because you've hit a ceiling? Are you struggling financially? Or do you see a more efficient path to growth and realizing your vision?

You want to be careful here. Potential buyers are always going in with the lens of "What is wrong with this business?" You want to avoid feeding that worry.

The facts are always the facts. But the way you deliver them is what makes all the difference.

Buyer Qualifications

What qualifications should acceptable buyers have? Who are you interested in speaking to about them? Who is a good fit? Will you just be wasting their time?

Directions for the LOI

What steps should the viewers take to show interest in acquiring your startup? Whom exactly should they contact to begin the conversation and ask questions, and how should they contact them?

6

Putting Your Finances in Order

GETTING YOUR FINANCES IN ORDER is a critical step in M&A. The sooner you do it, the better.

This foundational step is vital for a smooth and efficient M&A process. Putting your finances in order will help you and your team get clarity on where you really stand as a company and acquisition target. It will be the basis for valuations. It will help you sail through and survive due diligence and know who your best target buyers are. It will also shine a light on what your alternative options may be, while best preparing bankers and advisors to do their jobs well. It can also help you create a strong, accurate, and effective pitchbook.

This is about organizing financial documents and having clarity on your own real numbers—something that will also help you optimize your finances and financial structure for potential buyers, as you'll discover in other sections of this book. Beyond presenting your company in the best light and with the best value possible, you'll be adding more value with fresh projections and financial models and preparing yourself and your team for the questions you'll be asked, from pre-LOI through to negotiations, due diligence, and closing.

This is about knowing the details, fine-tuning them, and the art of casting a vision of the value that could be.

Understanding Financials

You may or may not be a numbers geek. Many founders don't live and breathe for the finer financial details. They are visionaries, creatives, and doers. That's okay. Yet, this is one of those times when all founders, decision-makers, and those on the M&A committee really need to get in tune with the math and granular details of the numbers, financials, and metrics.

You have to know where you are, how that compares to buyer wants and expectations, and what your team can do to bridge the gap and bring your A game to the table.

Your team needs to have clarity, know the mission and messaging, and know how to answer the questions that are coming your way.

One of the first steps here is to get a detailed handle on your current finances and financial statements. You will need to provide new financial statements to potential buyers through your deal room. This information is also going to be used for your pitchbook and other marketing materials. Although you may not divulge too much up front as a private company, you have to ensure this is a good match and that expectations are aligned on both sides of the table. Otherwise, you are just wasting time.

The following financial documents will be front and center here:

- Previous years' financial statements
- Year-to-date profit-and-loss statement
- Balance sheet
- Previous years' tax returns
- Cash flow statement and analysis
- Financial projections

The Importance of Key Metrics

Different buyers put different priorities on various figures and metrics. These numbers can instantly tell potential buyers a lot about your business. They can also directly affect your valuation.

Although there are things you can do to make improvements on these metrics now, imperfect numbers can also signal opportunity and value-add potential for buyers who can come in and take it to the next level with their resources and expertise. In other cases, these metrics will rule out certain potential buyers, or make your company especially attractive to them, particularly when it comes to the difference between strategic and financial buyers.

Some of the key metrics in M&A will include burn rate, hard costs, EBITDA, gross revenues, gross profit margins, sales units, customer acquisition costs, growth rate, and debt to equity. The following sections take a closer look at these metrics.

Burn Rate

Burn rate is still very applicable and important in M&A today, especially when so many later-stage startups and public companies are still losing money—not because of any crisis, but because that's the way they designed it. So, how fast is your startup burning through money? If it isn't profitable, acquirers are going to need to carry that monthly debt obligation until they can turn it around or find another way to produce value from it.

Hard Costs

It is important to differentiate between fixed hard expenses and variable expenses that fluctuate with sales and may be easier to tweak and optimize. What overhead is there in terms of real estate loans or leases, insurance and licenses, maintenance, salaries, and so on?

EBITDA

Earnings before interest, taxes, depreciation, and amortization (EBITDA) is one of the most important metrics potential buyers will look at when it comes to M&A. It is particularly important for financial buyers. This metric shows the cash flow after most fixed costs and variable expenses. In addition to cash flow, it also gives insight into how profitable the company is in relationship to its spending. Strong buyers may be able to take your company and restructure financing and taxes, creating far more profitability on the same earnings.

Gross Revenues

Gross revenues show the total cash coming into the business. Many buyers will be able to restructure expenses and costs under this to greatly improve profitability, though existing revenues give them a real, tangible figure they can use to evaluate the deal, justify it, and finance it. Any additional revenues they can add on top are icing on the cake. This volume also indicates what level of company it is and what buyers may be interested.

Gross Profit Margins

Gross profit margin is an easy-to-insert metric, even for early-stage startups in their forward-looking projections. It's a very telling number that instantly reveals whether the company is in the right ballpark for their industry—or that reveals big issues that wouldn't otherwise be expected. Gross profit margin in forecasts for pre-revenue startups immediately shows whether founders are on the right track or if they're out of touch with their industry.

For example, if you are forecasting 60 percent gross revenues in an industry that typically struggles to maintain a 35 percent margin, either you have created something truly amazing with a lot of value, or you are overlooking a lot of the expenses. In the reverse, if you are forecasting 35 percent gross margins in a space where investors and financiers expect at least 60 percent, then you may also be hitting your head against a wall, and you need to go back under the hood and rework your idea.

Sales Units

How many units are you selling? Have you proven product-market fit? Are you still an early-stage startup with tens of thousands of units being sold each year? Or are you a mature business with millions of units sold each year? This not only indicates the best type and level of buyer but also how accurate you have been with early predictions, and it indicates the potential of the company.

Customer Acquisition Costs

This is one of the most pivotal metrics for startups. One of the riskiest factors for businesses is customer acquisition costs. High costs here not only mean low profit margins and questionable unit economics but also signal great risk—especially if current channels falter or those costs rise further. For some acquirers, target companies with high customer acquisition costs can indicate ripe opportunities. An M&A deal could enable them to plug your product into their infrastructure and channels and dramatically boost sales units, with almost zero additional customer acquisition costs.

Growth Rate

Growth is one of the top drivers of acquisitions and mergers. So how fast are you growing? The earlier the stage, the higher the expectations are for growth. At the earliest stages, young startups may be reporting growth on a week-over-week basis. Later on, it will be month over month. Eventually, more mature companies will be tracking and reporting quarterly and annually. How much growth is left can be a big deal, too.

Debt to Equity

The debt-to-equity ratio shows how solvent the company truly is and what real equity there is to acquire. Debt may be restructured by new acquirers and parent companies, or startups may wish to settle debts ahead of an acquisition. This is especially true if it's questionable whether new owners will have potential issues assuming any loans and credit. Current debt also shows how well the company has done at servicing any credit it's used and is a good indicator for leveraged buyouts and private equity buyers.

Why Growth and Operating Assumptions Are Critical

A significant part of valuation and driving an M&A transaction is the forecasts for growth and operating expenses.

There is a huge difference in what your company may be tangibly worth right now, with its current assets, income, liabilities, and verifiable financial track record, and what it could be worth five years from now, in the right hands.

If you only get offered what it is worth to a financial buyer simply in a conventional sense right now, not everyone in your organization may be thrilled. Yet, there is a chance to dramatically increase the perceived value of your company by forecasting where you will be as a standalone venture on your current trajectory and as a part of a new merged company.

The difference between these figures can be night and day for current shareholders, potential acquirers, and founders. For buyers, these projections can make all the difference in the perceived value and sense of urgency. They may not be able to pay you what the company could be worth five years from now. This is their chance to buy low and reap the rewards, either from what they can add or the growth your venture brings in terms of customer count, market share, revenues, cash flow, and profit and returns.

Be bold with your forecasts and vision. Be optimistic. Think big. Show the possibility.

Just make sure that your big claims and projections are anchored in logic. Be aggressive, but be able to back up those claims with facts and figures.

Your financial modeling will need to be backed by authoritative research. Although financial projections may be rough and lean for early-stage startups, they still need to be based on solid assumptions supporting your growth and operational cost claims. This is vital for the following three main reasons.

Assumptions Are the Basis for All of Your Other Financials

Detailed underlying assumptions should include figures for growth in total available market and operational expenses including salaries and cost of goods sold. If your assumptions on these foundation factors are deeply flawed, then the end calculations will be way off, too. Make sure you can link to authoritative research and statistics to back up your claims. Be sure to factor in variables such as inflation, especially on items such as raw materials, shipping, and payroll.

Credibility

You might win some points for passion, charisma, optimism, and thinking big when fundraising, but when it comes to M&A, your credibility relies on fact and your track record of what you've been able to actually achieve. If you are just picking growth numbers out of the sky, then don't expect a lot of your other claims to be taken seriously. If you clearly haven't done your homework and checked your numbers, you can expect them to want to look doubly hard at everything else in due diligence—but if they try to question and fact-check you, and you can back up your assumptions with strong data, they are going to assume you've been just as diligent in other areas of your business.

Earnouts

You may be able to add a lot of perceived value for strategic buyers with great forecasts alone. Of course, they are going to want to tie a large percentage of the price to you being able to deliver on that. You may end up staying on, in charge of delivering on those projections for the next three years—at least if you want the other half of your money. Don't promise more than you are confident you can deliver.

Modeling Out a Powerful Five-Year Projection

A core part of your financials and presentation in M&A is going to be your forward-facing five-year financial projections.

Depending on the scenario and the buyers who are courting your business, this may be a projection of your business as a standalone entity and its future performance and/or projections of what your company and assets could look like in the hands of this new buyer, with the latter having the potential to be many times greater than what you can achieve on your own, even with raising more capital. Be sure to consult your M&A advisors here. To effectively forecast what you could achieve together, you must be sure you understand what the buyer intends to do with your business and why it is really buying you. Otherwise, you will be totally off-base or potentially selling yourself out of hundreds of millions or billions of dollars.

With this modeling, you can identify *hard synergies*, which represent cost savings, and *soft synergies*, which are potential revenue increases. There may be other factors as well, depending on the reasoning for acquiring you. You want to show how you are meeting their goals—and, more specifically, how you are going to help them meet their goals more efficiently and with greater value than acquiring one of your competitors instead.

The basics for five-year financial projections can be found in the three-statement model:

1. Income statement
2. Balance sheet
3. Cash-flow statement

You'll build one for you as the target company and one from the perspective of the acquiring company.

These financial statements should link to your underlying assumptions and be dynamic in nature so that adjustments and various alternative scenarios can be viewed on-the-fly to avoid losing time or deals.

If you are an Excel ninja, then you may find this relatively fast and easy to put together and then review and navigate with your team. Or you can choose a more modern startup and M&A-specific financial modeling tool.

Anticipating Questions on Numbers

The ability to present well and having a good sales game is great, but it is only going to stick if you're also prepared to answer the questions you're going to get in the follow-up.

The following are some common questions that you can expect to encounter:

- Is any existing debt assumable?
- Are there any community or charity obligations to be assumed?
- How much of the purchase price are you willing to bet on to achieve projections?
- If your numbers are so good, why would you be willing to sell?
- Are there any new regulatory fees that can be expected in the near future?
- Who prepared these financials?
- How did you arrive at your assumptions?

7

Understanding Your Valuation

HOW MUCH IS YOUR COMPANY worth? How will buyers be coming up with a valuation for your business?

If you pay attention to the stories promoted by media organizations, multibillion dollar exits may sound like the new normal. That is certainly a milestone to shoot for. Yet, in reality, as of this writing, the average exit price is still about $200 million. It is definitely nothing to be ashamed of if you are selling your company for millions.

You certainly don't want to undersell yourself, your company, or your investors and team. You don't want to sell yourself short of (potentially) billions of dollars. But you don't want to ask for far too much and have serious buyers dismiss you because they think you are being unrealistic.

You also probably have a legal responsibility to other shareholders. You need to be able to show them how valuations work, what is fair, and when they may be foolish—or even crazy—to turn down an offer.

So what is a startup worth?

The simple answer is this: whatever someone is willing to pay for it at any given time.

There is also an art to valuing startups. There are common mathematical equations others will apply to your business as well.

Variables Affecting Your Startup's Value

These are just some of the variables that can be used to calculate what your company may be worth and the offers you can expect and demand.

- Current market and economic conditions
- The company buying you
- The competition over acquiring your company
- Method of payment (cash or stock)
- The terms, including earnouts, vesting and resting, and so on
- Recent valuations of your company at fundraising rounds
- The moat you have built around your business or lack of it
- How organized and prepared you and your documents are
- The strengths or weaknesses of relationships with potential acquirers
- What a new buyer can do with your company and its parts

How well you position your startup and how well you do at selling it, including the strength of your pitchbook and story, can make a big difference in maximizing an exit, too.

Common Methods of Business Valuation

Startups that already have established revenues and profits are relatively straightforward to value. There are several traditional ways to do that, especially when it comes to acquisitions by financial buyers. The following sections explore some of the ways you may choose a figure for your startup.

Your Number

If you have other shareholders, then you have legal responsibilities to them. You cannot just fire sell your company without their input or turn down good offers without their approval.

However, it is worth having your own number in mind. Even though it always makes sense to get outside advice, if you don't have to get the approval of other stakeholders, then you should have a number that makes sense to take.

For first-time entrepreneurs, this isn't about winning the M&A lottery and acquiring an obscene amount of wealth on your first exit. It may be about walking away with a life-changing sum that will take finances off of your mind. An amount that will ensure you don't have to worry about being broke or homeless or not being able to retire (if you ever want to). You may be looking for enough to do everything you want for your children and family and to give them opportunities. You may want an amount that will enable you to go on to other projects and focus on what you want to solve and change because you can, not because you need the money.

Just make sure you are genuinely getting enough to give you a good return on all of the time, energy, and money you've put in—unless you really need to fire sell your company and just get out what you can.

Earnings Multiples

Publicly traded and mature businesses are typically traded on multiples of their earnings. This is a comfortable method that Wall Street uses and a default way of comparing companies on the fly.

The big problem with this approach for many startup companies is that they have no meaningful earnings or net profit. Even if *you* do, it may not really reveal your true potential, especially to a strategic buyer who can dramatically multiply those earnings overnight.

The Comparables Approach

On the surface, this can be one of the simplest methods to understand and calculate on the spot. It can be even simpler for smaller, more traditional businesses—especially those that may turn to business brokers to advertise and sell their companies.

Like valuing a house, it is about looking at what other similar companies in your space with similar size are selling for.

For example, if another Amazon seller in your niche with similar financials just sold their business for $X, then yours is also worth $X, plus or minus any variances. Other adjustments may be made by user count, recent IPOs of similar companies, and so on.

Cost to Replicate

How much would it cost someone else to simply duplicate what you've built? If a bigger company wanted what you have, how much would it cost the company in time, money, hiring, and risk to replicate it and get it to the same stage?

Ideally, buying you is the cheaper, faster, and least risky option.

Discounted Cash Flow Method

This approach creates a forecast of potential cash flow for a specific time period or life of the company, factors in a desired return on investment (ROI), and applies a discount to factor in risk. The earlier stage the startup is, the higher the risk for the buyer, and the deeper the discount will be.

Additional Valuation Methods

Other business valuation approaches include the following:

- Berkus method (assumes a specific revenue by year five, assigns values to specific line items, and determines an overall value and return for investors)

- Venture capital method (projects future revenues, assigns a trading multiple to estimated net profits, and provides a desired return)
- Book value (evaluates the tangible value of existing assets)
- The scorecard valuation method (ranks a startup based on multiple factors, including team strength, opportunity size, sales channels, and so on)

How to Value Pre-revenue Startups

There are plenty of pre-revenue startups, and even those losing sizable amounts of money every year get bought or go public. So, what are the methods that can specifically apply to early-stage, pre-revenue startups? What can you do to increase your valuation?

Traditionally, the most desired method of valuation has been based on EBITDA. It is about the income, just like a dividend-paying public stock or rental property.

Of course, it can be quite a while before your startup has revenues if you haven't prioritized that out of the gate. That doesn't mean you can't enjoy a big exit.

If you are still pre-revenue, the common methods of valuing startups at your stage include the Berkus method, the venture capital method, the scorecard method, risk factor summation, and the First Chicago method. The following sections take a quick look at each of these approaches.

The Berkus Method

The Berkus method assumes a startup will have $20 million in revenue by year five. It assigns a value of up to $500,000 for five line items. This gives a new pre-revenue startup up to $2.5 million in value and almost a 10× return for investors.

Values are assigned to these factors and summed up:

- Business idea
- Having a prototype

- Strength of the management team
- Strategic relationships
- Having rolled out a product or starting sales

Venture Capital Method

This method begins by projecting future revenues (for example, five years from now), assigning a trading multiple to estimated net profits based on industry benchmarks, and then providing the desired return for an investor.

The Scorecard Method

This valuation method uses comparable companies at the same stage in the same industry and region as a base point.

Simply put, theoretically, if your startup is identical to another that was just valued at $10 million, then yours should be worth $10 million, too. The scorecard method then adjusts the value of the subject startup based on the following factors:

- Strength of management
- Size of opportunity
- Product/tech
- Competitive environment
- Marketing and sales
- Need for additional capital
- Miscellaneous factors

Risk Factor Summation

This method of valuation looks at 12 risk factors and adds or subtracts monetary value on a five-point scale from very high risk to very low risk for each one:

- Potential exit
- Reputation

- International
- Litigation
- Technology
- Competition
- Funding
- Sales and marketing
- Manufacturing
- Legislation
- Stage of business
- Management

First Chicago Method

This valuation method bases the future value of a startup on its projected cash flow. It is effectively a discounted cash flow model (as already described in this chapter). It also moderates these projections, balancing worst-case, base-case, and best-case financial projections.

How to Increase Your Valuation Faster

If you aren't excited about your potential value after using these methods and calculations, what can you do to take control of it and accelerate your value ahead of an exit?

Improve Your Pitch

The art of a great exit often comes down to being able to cast a great vision, present it well, and sell the idea of what could be. Once you put your mind to it, you may be surprised at how much your company could be worth in the right hands.

Get Those Revenues In

If you feel that a lack of revenues, or limited revenues, is a roadblock to the exit you want and need, then start selling.

Your startup is at a whole new level when you have proof of commercial viability and product-market fit.

Another great avenue to take is to begin selling to your potential acquirers' customers. When they see the fit with their customers, you've taken a lot of risk and uncertainty off the table, and that adds a lot of value.

Get Your Prototype or Minimum Viable Product Done Today

You might have a great team, technology, and vision, but without a tangible product, you haven't proven you can take it over the finish line and unlock its real value. Stop over-engineering it and get it out in the world.

Build Out Your Team

The quality of your team alone could be the reason you are acquired and where buyers see most of the value. Hire better executives, key team leaders, and the best talent in your space. This can add a lot of benefits to your business in the meantime, too.

Typically, the acquisitions that are focused on a team are, for the most part, called *acquihires*, when the actual business itself takes a step back from an interest perspective. Acquihires typically happen when the acquiring company sees the opportunity to speed up the hiring process by bringing onboard an already assembled team that it can repurpose to something else. Acquihires are a great way to accelerate the onboarding of talent by recruiting groups of individuals at the same time as opposed to recruiting employees one by one.

Position Your Startup in the Right Way

Remember that M&A is about the buyer's perception. When fundraising, you often have to reposition your startup to match what different investors are about.

For example, you may have a biotech startup doing something revolutionary for women. For one investor, you may highlight the tech side. For another, the science. Another may be more passionate about funding female founders or the impact investment aspect.

The same is true when it comes to acquirers. This enables you to benchmark your startup valuation against a very different set of companies.

Valuation versus Terms

Valuation has its place, though experienced founders will tell you that they would prefer to let the buyer pick the price, if they can choose the terms.

The details, terms, and fine print can make far more of a difference in the net and the ultimate outcome. This is especially true for founders.

The terms lay out important factors such as types of shares, clauses that come along with vesting, earnouts, and other rules of the deal. In fact, sometimes a lower valuation can be preferred and prove more profitable over a higher one.

Know what a fair and attractive valuation is, but don't get hung up on it. Don't allow it to hide the real underlying math and conditions.

Why You Never Want to Disclose Your Valuation

You will be performing your own audit, calculations, valuation, and financial modeling in advance. You want to know how others will value your company according to these different methods ahead of time.

To start, you want to make sure you can really expect a number in the ballpark of what makes sense for you and your shareholders and is acceptable to your investors. You also want to be sure you aren't being taken advantage of and can speak knowledgeably about these valuation methods.

However, you don't want to disclose this valuation or range of valuations to your potential acquirers or to the public.

If the transaction remains private, your acquirer may not want the price made public in the news. Don't sabotage your own deal before it gets done.

You also don't want to show your hand in advance of negotiations. Let buyers pitch their offers first. They may be thinking of a number hundreds of millions or billions more than you are thinking.

They can have a whole different perspective on why they need you and what this deal could be worth. Your acquirer can also add an incredible amount of value to your company overnight.

Avoiding High Valuations with No Rationale

If you've read *The Art of Startup Fundraising* or raised a few rounds of financing with great advisors around you, then you already know that higher valuations aren't always better.

If you start floating your own extreme valuation demands, serious buyers may dismiss you and go right to the competition they think is reasonably priced or at least is still in touch with reality.

If you end up switching from M&A mode back to trying to fundraise, then higher-than-needed valuations can make things more difficult in the future. They can even create more issues internally.

If there is really no solid math behind an extraordinary valuation, then the deal may not stick. Sooner or later someone in the process is going to call it out. They have legal responsibilities to their investors, too.

Don't drive your valuation too low, either. Whether this deal happens or not, these valuations can influence your ability and the terms of being able to acquire other businesses. That can be crucial to your overall growth and profitability.

Although it may seem superficial, valuation also has a very real impact on your appeal and credibility as a company. This can make a big difference when it comes to hiring, recruiting advisors, getting press, drawing other investors, and even in who wants to become a customer and how much they are willing to pay for your product or services.

8

Building the Target List

FUNDRAISING FOR YOUR STARTUP AND focusing on the best investors, selling your company and positioning it, and crafting a winning pitchbook are all about considering and targeting the ideal shortlist of buyers for the optimal outcome.

Some entrepreneurs have become especially talented at consistently forging new startups and crafting them from the beginning to be acquired by a specific buyer or group of buyers. They design everything with the exit in mind before they launch. They can be in and out and create immense value and impact in a very short period of time.

It is worth noting that this is the rare exception rather than the common path. Most don't have this kind foresight and experience. Most first-time entrepreneurs don't think this far ahead. Generally those who do start with big aspirations of creating a startup to sell it for big numbers don't get it right when it comes to predicting their most likely acquirer on the first try (at least not from the time that they are pitching their seed round).

No matter at what point you are reading this on your journey—whether you've just started researching your first venture to get ahead of the game, or you're facing a fork in the road, or you're under pressure to find an exit and you're creating your pitchbook—building a target list of buyers is smart and extremely valuable.

The Importance of Building the Target List

What's so important about taking the time to build a list of potential buyers for your company? Aren't companies bought, not sold? What if you already have inbound interest? What if investment bankers want to help out with the process?

In all of these scenarios, building a target list is still highly relevant.

You want to be able to optimize your business to attract these potential acquirers, draw the best offers, and have the right stuff to shop your company and generate competing bids, even if you get a great offer out of the blue.

Following are just some of the benefits of investing a little time in building your target list.

Not Alienating Ideal Buyers

Knowing your buyers means not burning capital, not devaluing your company, and not creating animosity between your teams in advance. It means not creating "assets" with no additional value for them. It also means not tearing them down in the press.

Saving Time

There are plenty of demands on your time during the daily course of business. There will be even more once you begin the M&A process.

The last thing you need is to waste time talking to all the wrong buyers—or worse, getting tied up with them and divulging sensitive information when it isn't going to be a great fit anyway.

This isn't like fundraising when you may be willing to talk to 300 potential investors and pitch them to get a deal, especially when anticipating selling for the largest dollar amounts. You will probably be limiting conversations to a handful of acquirers. Make sure you are talking to the right ones.

Maximizing the Price

If you know who your target buyers are, then you can curate your company for them and your pitchbook. Pay attention to the way you present and highlight what you have and the value for them. What can you de-risk and prove to them to justify a bigger price tag?

Achieving the Best Terms

Being able to curate your company for a target list means being in the position to negotiate better terms and even making them obvious to offer. This can include how they pay, how long they'll demand founders stay on, and more.

Optimal Outcome for Your Team

If you truly care about your team, then you want to find an acquirer who is going to create the best outcome for them as well. That may be financial in the short term, meaningful roles in the medium term, and packages that give them long-term security and opportunities.

Best Future for Your Mission and Product

Targeting your buyers means knowing who will truly be the best fit to carry on the mission, vision, and impact you wanted and who will make the most of the work and products you've created.

Efficiency in the M&A Process

A tight target list means greater efficiency throughout the process. It means not having to divert your teams and burn hours and months creating the wrong materials or pushing unnecessary projects.

ROI on Your Deal-Making Efforts

Whether it is labor hours, your personal time, any commissions, or other investments, a tighter list means a better ROI across the board.

Ways to Identify Potential Buyers

When you want to build your target list, you need to understand your own organization's needs in this process, and then you need to know what traits and criteria you're looking for in potential buyers. To determine who is justified being on your target list, consider the factors in the following sections.

Why Are You Selling?

Which buyers are the best matches for your goals and priorities in this exit? Whether financial or mission-focused, which three to five companies are the best fit?

What Type of Buyer Is the Right Fit?

What types of buyers are the best fit for the stage your company is in and are the most likely candidates to want to acquire you? What motivators are in play that signal these buyers? Are they big strategic or financial buyers and institutions? Or are they other startups?

Culture Fit

Which of these companies offers the best culture fit? This is going to be key to successful integration and the longevity of your work, your team's jobs, and even the ability to ride out any earn-out periods.

Ability to Buy

To make your shortlist, they have to have the financial ability to buy you. Do they have enough cash or equity? Do they have the credit and connections if they will be financing the purchase?

Motivation

Who has enough motivation and the sense of urgency to acquire you? Just like any investor or customer, corporate buyers aren't going to take the action to initiate the process, much less follow through with the process (because of the time it requires), unless they are really motivated.

Competence in M&A

Who is capable of efficiently and effectively pulling off the deal? These deals can be complicated. Some organizations have existing processes and systems and have done it a dozen times. Others may end up using you and your transaction as their first guinea pig.

Trust and Alignment of Values

Ability is great, and so is an attractive offer on paper that checks most of your boxes, but whom do you trust to do what they say to follow through before and after the closing? Who has the values you believe will guide them to do the right thing?

Vetting Buyers for the Right Fit

You should be doing just as much vetting of your buyers as they want to complete on you. This isn't just basic business sense—it will also play well to that buyer that you really care about whom you are selling to, that there is a match, and that you aren't just dumping your company on the first buyer you can.

Research

There is a lot of basic research your teams can do in this process. Your other competitive research, SWOT analysis, and fundraising prep should hold plenty of clues as to where to start looking.

You can easily hit the web to find out the most active acquirers in your space. You can also find out who has recently raised capital, and you can uncover red flags of companies you may not want to engage with.

Some of the online tools you can use for research include the following:

- Crunchbase
- PitchBook
- CB Insights
- Owler

M&A Professionals

Business brokers, investment bankers, and advisors can all hold significant inside knowledge. They also have the potential to make important introductions. Essentially, this is the role we play at Panthera Advisors and how we provide value.

Interview Others

Just as it is smart to talk to other founders who have raised money from investors before accepting capital from anyone, it can be very revealing to have conversations with other founders who have sold to these companies. The process of engaging a conversation can also say a lot. What worked? What didn't? What should you expect from following the process? What shouldn't you expect?

To find out more, you can also listen to episodes of my *DealMakers* podcast, where entrepreneurs share how their companies were acquired for millions (or billions).

Remember that history always repeats. Don't try to reinvent the wheel. See what works for others and take out a page from their stories to apply to your own path.

Build Personal Relationships

Everyone talks a good game. Anyone can fool everyone for a little while, but people can't fool everyone forever.

Building personal relationships can open doors, but those relationships give you a whole new level of insight into the individuals and company you'll be dealing with. Those connections will also be the stickiness that keeps them honest after the deal closes and through all the rough patches in between.

Become a Customer or Vendor

Many business relationships end up morphing into something even bigger. This is also often where you'll find strategic acquirers in your space.

If you are a customer of theirs or a vendor to them, it will show you a lot about how the company really does business. You'll see the reality of how the company operates, lives up to its promises, and how competent and efficient it is—at a level you'll only get by doing business with the company over time.

Partner Up

Going even deeper, partnering up with different potential acquirers is another way to really learn about people and test out how things may work in a merger or acquisition. The following section explores the power of partnerships in more detail.

Using Partnerships to Trigger Acquisitions

Partnerships with other companies are not only a great way to grow your business and test out potential acquirers but also they're a powerful tool to trigger acquisitions—in particular, inbound offers. (They make acquirers feel it's their idea.) The process through integration can go much, much more smoothly in these scenarios, too. I have personally seen acquisitions in the hundreds of millions done in just days.

Whom should you partner with? It makes sense to build your target list first and then choose partners.

Who else is up, down, and sideways in your space and would eventually want to expand their ownership of the supply chain, geographic area, or technology and products, which makes acquiring you the next logical step for them to think of?

Show them the benefits through de-risking investments in technology, recruiting teams, product development, and expansion.

Show them how much cheaper, easier, and faster it is to acquire you over re-creating these things themselves. Model the outcomes of returns and growth from partnering together.

Show how much better it is for them to own you compared to the alternative of competing against you. And what if you move on to merge with one of their competitors?

Following are some of the types of partnerships to consider:

- Cross-selling products
- Bundling services
- Licensing them your technology
- Combining the use of teams, tech, premises, and equipment
- Building new products together
- Collaborating on marketing initiatives and events

- Joint venture investments
- Limited-time exclusive referral agreements

How to Make Contact with Interested Parties

When you have your target list of potential acquirers, how do you go about getting in touch with them? Figure 8.1 shows a good 30,000-foot view of how to make contact with interested parties.

The following sections explore each of the ways of making contact in more detail.

Introductions and Referrals

Introductions and referrals are still the best way to meet people. This is especially true when the stakes are significant and trust and credibility are determining factors in getting a conversation and being taken seriously.

Depending on the size of the organization, there are several parties you may talk to and several paths to take. The higher up you can enter the conversation, usually the better it is. The people you talk to may be the executive team, the founders, or the CEO. It may be an investor on the board who has the ear of the founder, who is

Figure 8.1 How to Make Contact with Interested Parties

also motivated to find an exit. Or it could be someone in a dedicated acquisitions team.

Who knows the people you need to connect with and has a relationship with them? Who has a Rolodex with these people's names?

Networking

Personal networking is a great way to make direct connections and can include professional and organized networking events. (You can always host if you're looking for an event with the right attendee list.)

Casual networking is also an option. Where do these people hang out when they aren't in the office? Is there a certain happy hour you are likely to find them at? Do they have a favorite ski resort, hotel in Cabo, marina, or yacht show? Be there.

Cold Emails

Cold calling still works. In this realm, however, an email is obviously a lot more likely to get through than a phone call. Email is still the preferred method of professional communication. It works for fundraising, and it can work for M&A, too.

Other channels where you can try cold outreach include LinkedIn and Twitter.

Never underestimate the power of social media. I have a friend who sold his company for $150 million, and it happened via a cold message that he received from the acquirer on LinkedIn.

Be So Good They Can't Ignore You

You can accomplish two goals at once by getting noticed. Use that attention to get their attention and trigger the motivation and interest in acquiring you.

Use the press to make noise about what your company is doing and the traction you are gaining. Publish reports and articles on what's next for your industry and trigger people into needing to take action.

If you are ready, push forward toward an IPO or your next fund-raising round. This can often result in conversations turning toward buying you.

As an example, I interviewed Jyoti Bansal on the *DealMakers* podcast. The announcement of his startup's acquisition happened within just hours of going public. His company, AppDynamics, ended up getting acquired by Cisco for $3.7 billion.

In Jyoti's case, the IPO scenario created an incredible fear of missing out for Cisco, and they ended up paying the price necessary to get them off that track. It was the perfect timing and a great execution by the AppDynamics team.

Move Up the List in Reverse Order

Move up your target list in reverse order. Start working the last potential buyer on the list first. Put the least desirable acquirer on your shortlist.

This strategy has two powerful benefits. First, you will be able to listen and learn a lot about what the people on the other side of the table are looking for, and this can dramatically improve your pitch, presentation, and answers by the time you get to talk to those at the top of the list.

Second, each of these meetings can turn into a referral and introduction to others on your list or meetings with people you may have overlooked.

Use Brokers

Depending on the size of your business and the anticipated exit, there are a variety of types of dealmakers and brokers who can help, from lawyers to business brokers, bankers, and M&A consultants. Interview them; see how they can help you and what value they can offer.

The Golden Rule in Making Contact

In virtually all of these situations, you are not just raising your hand or waving a for sale sign. You want it to be their idea. You approach them for advice, with the potential to work together, or to add value to them in some way.

Keep in mind that they should be the ones to make the first move when it comes to starting the conversation about buying your business.

9

The Communication Process with Buyers

What are the best practices for communicating with potential acquirers of your business and carrying those conversations over the finish line—or at least, to the next phase of real negotiations and making a deal?

This can be a very delicate process, where every word matters when it comes to offers and negotiations. This is also a period in which you can completely blow great opportunities or create surprisingly good outcomes.

This stage is about carefully nurturing potential interest in an M&A transaction, ensuring you are engaging with and speaking to the right people, and identifying the real motivations of a potential buyer and how you can position a deal for the maximum results.

Liabilities and Responsibilities

At this stage of a venture, these conversations and deals are no longer about you and your personal finances.

You may definitely have a voice and vote and the option to negotiate a fair and attractive exit package for yourself as a shareholder.

Yet, if you have cofounders, equity investors, creditors, and others with stock options, the equation becomes about them and the health and benefit of the corporation itself.

There can be serious legal responsibilities, with legal liability for mistakes made, negligence, and failing to act in line with your assumed fiduciary responsibility.

Even without other legal shareholders, you may feel a responsibility to your employees, customers, and other supporters who have backed your mission. You want the best for them and the company, even if you will be taking a step back from it in the near future.

With these things in mind, every communication has a certain level of importance.

How to Handle Communications

Your legal counsel will have some input on how to handle M&A-related conversations. You may be soliciting advice from your own personal attorney and corporate attorneys.

In some cases, they may tell you that phone conversations are good when no legal agreements are being made.

Provided conversations are not being recorded, parties can't hold anything against you or claim you committed to a certain deal or terms. (Of course, you don't want to be accused of saying something you didn't, either.)

Email provides a clearly documented paper trail that holds all parties accountable—which can have its pros and cons.

Just be sensitive to the legal side here and keep it in mind when discussing any material aspects of a deal, terms, or when representing data and facts.

Vague conversations are fine, but defer any decisions on paperwork to your legal team and only provide solid answers on data when it can be verified.

Gauging Initial Interest

How do you go about gauging initial interest with potential buyers?

Inbound calls are pretty obvious. If you are doing the right things for your business and with an exit in mind, they will come. You might not take them seriously at first. You might think a call is a prank and hang up. That's okay.

On the *DealMakers* podcast, I remember interviewing Ray Reddy. During our interview, he talked about receiving a random email from Google that initially looked like spam. That email led to an acquisition worth millions.

At the end of the day, if potential acquirers are really serious, they will call back. Don't be rude. Don't take the outreach for granted. (But, in more than one case, turning down the first offer has landed entrepreneurs much bigger follow-up offers.)

This really comes down to the strength of your position, your legal responsibilities to others, and how much you are willing to bet on them coming back to you versus buying one of your competitors.

If anything, you can turn a mediocre inbound offer or conversation into a chance to shop and auction your business to others.

If you haven't yet received any cold inbound interest, then be on the lookout for responses to your marketing, PR, conversations, and any fundraising pitching and selling you are doing.

In other scenarios, comments about buying you or merging may be loosely thrown around in a conversation. Don't write them off. There could be something there if you follow up.

If you are just spending time with other executives or presenting demos and the topic of a "strategic partnership" comes up, don't let it slip away.

If they joke about buying you or merging, you can spark that train of thought in their minds. "Oh, yeah? What would that look like?" Or you can tempt them with, "If only you could afford us!" Or "Someone is probably going to buy us, especially when X happens."

Above all, in these conversations, you want to be sure you are attracting the right type of interest. The buyers with the right motivations. Parties that are really interested in a deal, not just milking information or distracting you.

A big part of gauging this initial interest will come out of whom they send to talk to you and whether or not there is an obvious synergy or alignment in getting a deal done, versus hampering your business.

Nailing the Follow-Up

If you've had vague inbound interest, real inquiries, or you've sparked some conversations with executives at partner companies, or you've generated interest with your pitchbook after shopping your startup, follow-up is key.

It's much the same as any other sales situation, especially for high-ticket items or enterprise sales. Buying or selling a company is not like pulling through the drive-through of your favorite coffee chain or throwing your product up on Amazon. There's even more to it than buying or selling a new car or house.

Expect it to take time. Expect to have to follow-up multiple times. They used to say the average sale took seven "touches." That's why you get all those drip emails, autoresponder texts, the junk mail, social ads displayed in your feed, and the same YouTube, TV, and radio ad clips shown on loop.

With all this noise and evolving customer behaviors, in many cases, it may take 11 or more touches and engagements to get to a closed sale.

It's important to understand that nailing the follow-up isn't just about you following up. You need to be aware that customers have to go through a lot of phases on their end. You can help them do some of these things, either directly or indirectly. And some things they'll want or need to do on their own. Understanding the customer's process will help you as you follow up with them. The phases the customer needs to move through are described in the following sections.

Awareness and Discovery

In order to buy or even consider buying, companies have to discover you and become aware of you. They have to know your company and product exists. Then, they have to become aware that there may be potential or an opportunity for a deal and the ability to purchase your company.

Learning

As with making any new investment or purchase of something new in the market, you want to learn more about it. You look them up. You ask about them. You ask them questions and investigate the surrounding marketplace and technology.

Consideration

If what they learn reveals potential value and they still like you as a company or investment, this is the stage when they really begin considering if they should buy, how they would fund it, and what that would look like. They'll also weigh the pros and cons or risks and upside potential

Comparison Shopping

No one wants to be embarrassed by grossly overpaying for something or buying a dud, right? Most people today don't even buy a coffee, hotel stay, lunch, or toothbrush without comparison shopping online first. Who would make an 8-, 9-, 10-, or 11-figure investment without at least doing a similar amount of research? What other companies are in the space that may be bought? How do their reviews compare? What about the price and value?

Trust

Before a sale is made, they have to develop some amount of trust in you. At this level of the game, it's not just trust in your tech or business operations. It's also your leadership team and those who would be handling the M&A process.

Due Diligence

Trust, but verify. No matter how excited they are, they must verify everything. Some of this soft due diligence will be done up front, followed by a lot more detailed verification after a preliminary deal is struck and you have an LOI.

Negotiation

Even when they've made the mental decision they want to buy, they still want to make sure they are getting a deal and on terms that are attractive to them.

Until you have an LOI in hand with the suggested terms to get a deal done, you are still just flirting with each other or they are asking you out on a date. You haven't put a ring on it yet.

So how do you follow up and take this type of buyer through the customer journey to making an offer?

There are a couple of paths the journey can take. A lot depends on whether it's inbound interest, interest sparked by your efforts, as well as whether you are beginning the process yourself versus using a banker or broker from the start. There's also the question of who the buyer is and how big the company is (a startup versus a Fortune 500 company) and your prior relationship.

Assuming you are handling the direction of most of this follow-up yourself, some of the ways to proceed include the following.

Email There are a variety of ways to use email to follow up. If you have personal contacts with real dealmakers, it doesn't hurt to drop them a line or two now and again to re-trigger the conversation.

You can also leverage Gmail ads to show up in their inbox and help keep you top of mind. This will also keep positioning your company as one they should be taking under their umbrella as an asset.

Email newsletter updates can also be powerful. Add them to your best-fitting lists. If the individual(s) are already investors in your company, use that angle.

You may also want to create and send corporate newsletters that include vendors, partners, and others in your space. In a newsletter, it's easy to drop in metrics, company news, and industry news that makes it obvious they should be pursuing the conversation more deeply and sooner rather than later.

Social Media Updates Much of the same applies to social media as email. You can prioritize public social media updates that continue to position your company as an attractive acquisition. Post big data points, new partnerships and contracts, and upcoming developments.

You can use private social media groups that they may be a part of to post more business-relevant updates as well.

Or you can use social media to actually be social and reach out personally to others in the company and keep conversations going. DM them, like their posts, and ask questions.

Phone Conversations If you're both the type of people who actually answer the phone, then it certainly wouldn't hurt to just call and say hi to the lead contact or decision-maker. In this regard, the decision-maker is typically the CEO, the head of corporate development, the head of business development, or the person who leads the division that has direct synergies with your business.

You can ask the person directly if he or she has had any more thoughts about the idea. Or you can float a new idea you have for testing a partnership or collaboration.

You can be more subtle and ambiguous and ask for advice on upcoming decisions. Or you could simply try to arrange an opportunity where you can get together to develop a personal relationship further.

Maybe you are hosting an event, maybe you're in town and want a restaurant recommendation, or maybe you have extra tickets to a game.

Meetings M&A deals are traditionally the end result of multiple meetings, most of which have traditionally been in person.

Regardless of the immense travel time and cost burden involved, it doesn't hurt to have a series of lower-level meetings to explore the idea and present your pitchbook.

In truth, although online meetings do lack some of the personal connection we've had the luxury of in the past, virtual meetings are far more efficient and cost-effective for all sides.

This is important: When you do your follow-up, don't spam them to death. Always try to add value.

Finding the Decision-Maker

As with any type of sale, unless you are dealing with *the* decision-maker, you are typically just wasting your time.

Consider classic purchasing scenarios in which leaving out a key decision-maker in a sales presentation is virtually guaranteed to be a bust.

This isn't new. Those who've been around long enough to remember the days of cold calling or door-to-door sales might remember salespeople asking if the parents were home. Why? Because the kids in the house didn't have the power to make the choices. They didn't have their parents' checkbook, and they weren't the ones making the calls on buying a new vacuum cleaner or insurance.

In the case of car sales, home sales, or mortgages, salespeople don't want to have conversations without all the decision-makers in the room.

First, this enables them to read their prospects far better and tailor the pitch correctly. Second, it is just burning time unless a decision can be made on the spot at the end of the pitch.

If a person goes to the car dealer and gets super excited about the latest sports car, the salesperson is wasting their time if the spouse has that person on a tight budget and is insisting on getting a sensible minivan instead.

The whole process will have to start over again from scratch when the spouse can make it into the showroom. The same applies to buying or financing a home in which all buyers have to agree and sign to make it a legal contract.

A variety of people may heavily influence the ultimate decision to follow through with a merger or acquisition.

They may not all have the final say or a game-changing vote, but their input can make or break it. Or at least help rather than hurt. The further you get up the decision chain and convince the real dealmakers, the easier everything will go.

C-Suite Executives

Aside from other major shareholders, this is where the real decision-making power is.

If the founders and management are smart, and they've surrounded themselves with a good, well-aligned board and investors, and they have good relationships with them, then, if you win the C-suite, you can breeze through the vote.

You can imagine if Steve Jobs loved you and knew you personally and told his team he wanted them to buy and integrate you, the deal would probably get done.

Corporate Development

Big companies often have dedicated corporate development departments.

It's this department's job to be out there searching for deals every day. There is a good chance you'll first get an email or phone call from this group.

It may be of the department's own volition, or in some cases, it may be at the direction of someone higher up. The department is doing the legwork to research, set appointments, and see if there is a potential fit.

Advisors

Internal and external advisors can have a big impact, too. Founders and CEOs should be following their advisors' guidance. If you win the hearts and minds of these influencers, it can be an excellent path to the real decision-makers and an easier transaction.

Transaction Leads

Someone on the buy side will be tasked with taking the lead on the transaction, before, during, and after the close. The person may not carry the big decision power of CEOs, CFOs, and advisors, but he or she can certainly derail the deal if that person doesn't like you or doesn't see the attractiveness of the deal.

Business Unit Leaders

Once your company is acquired, it will be rolled into one of your buyer's business units. Business unit leaders are sometimes unaware of these deals being made or have little say in them. Yet they will greatly (if not totally) determine what happens to your company after the closing.

After the acquisition is complete, you want to have a good communication flow with business unit leaders because you need them up to speed in order to ensure a successful integration. Otherwise, the entire acquisition could end up being a failure and put in jeopardy any of the potential incentives for you and the team that were agreed on as part of the acquisition.

10

Preparing for a Successful First Meeting

After you've initiated or accepted conversations with a potential acquirer or merger partner, the next step is successfully nailing that first meeting.

At this point, you've identified your ideal or target acquirers or at least vetted those inbound inquiries to make sure they are a good fit. You've tested their interest, followed up intelligently, prepared a winning pitchbook, and have made sure you have a direct line of communication with real dealmakers who can make decisions.

Now it is time to arrange and prepare for a real meeting about this potential M&A deal. This crucial meeting can be make or break.

If things go well and they find synergy and love you, other future glitches and issues can be survived and forgiven. If you don't nail the first meeting, then it is unlikely you'll get a second. Even if you do, you will already be on the defensive and trying to force it to work from a less advantageous point.

Success here relies a lot on preparation and planning. This means being prepared with the right materials and data, being in the right mindset, and understanding the thinking of those on the other side of the table. You need to know the questions and answers.

You need to know how to run a meeting that has great flow and gives you the upper hand in negotiations. And you need to know how to close the meeting.

Don't miss the opportunity. Don't rush it and burn it because you aren't really ready.

Finding Out the Strategic Road Map of the Buyer

Knowing yourself is important. You have to know yourself as a person, as an entrepreneur and leader, and you need to deeply understand your company, team, and your position in your market.

Knowing your strengths, weaknesses, threats, and opportunities is a factor that will come into play in the days ahead with the type of deal you are willing to make and with which buyer.

More important in this situation, you have to know your buyer. The better you know your buyer as a company and all of its players, the more likely you are to score the LOI, achieve a higher valuation, and see the deal actually get closed.

Great exits are not accidents. Some may attribute luck to their startup's success. This point in the process happens to be one where you make your own "luck." This is where preparation meets opportunity, where the art of the deal and the ultimate outcome depend heavily on a variety of micro-subtleties and negotiation tactics.

Unless, of course, you just want to leave your entire future and the future of your company and team to the whim of the overgenerosity of your buyer.

Every micro detail can matter when it comes to these first meetings. Don't stress yourself out over engineering them, but don't lose out by overlooking the power you have to influence the outcome.

You Have to Understand the Buyer

Understanding the strategic road map of the buyer begins with first understanding the buyer. Because companies are still made up of people, this means understanding their thinking at a corporate level and as individuals.

As part of the previous step (learning about the decision-makers and players involved in an M&A transaction), you should have begun to identify the individuals involved at the specific company.

If you are working on a very tight shortlist of buyers, narrowing it down to a real meeting, you want to know these individuals by name. You want to know as much about them as individuals as possible. Every edge you can get for these negotiations can help.

This will help to avoid detractors who may shortsightedly derail the deal or make it much more difficult and make the terms less attractive.

You want to know the executives, board members, major shareholders, key team members and cofounders, relevant department heads, transaction coordinators, advisors, bankers, attorneys, and corporate development leads.

A little research into these individuals can reveal a lot. Just reading their bios and résumés, and taking a glance at their LinkedIn, Twitter, and Instagram profiles, can tell you more than you expect. These steps can unveil their world view, passions and frustrations, backstory and experiences, who is in their network that you might know, and even their favorite colors, meals, and what they are reading.

You may also discover information about their personal strategies. That's a lot you can work with when it comes to curating a meeting and tailoring a presentation. You can connect with them better and lay out the opportunity in a way that appeals to them personally as much as it checks the boxes at the corporate level.

The Importance of the Buyer's Strategic Road Map

Understanding the buyer and the company's strategic road map is pivotal to connecting on the right points in the right way. The strategic road map can apply to this specific deal and your company, the transition and post-transition, and the company as a whole in the short, medium, and long term.

Your understanding of this is critical to checking their boxes as well as maximizing perceived value. It will also help you gain better expectations of how the acquisition or merger process will unveil itself and how fast you might expect to close.

Specifically, it will also help you do the following:

- Manage the perception of exclusivity in what they are looking for and what you can offer
- Decide how to manage the phasing of information
- Maintain the right pace of momentum
- Deliver on the buyer's tolerance and need for risk-reward balance
- Be sure you are competitively positioned
- Establish synergies
- Present optionality
- Highlight how you are the best choice for a successful integration

How Do You Learn More about the Buyer's Strategic Road Map?

Asking questions is a good start. Start with your initial frontline contact. Why is the company interested in buying you? What is the pitch the company plans to take to the team to sell the deal? How does this specifically fit into the company's current strategic plans, goals, and needs?

Dig into the data. What has this company been up to? What track is it on? Or what challenges is it facing that it needs to buy your company to overcome? Who is influencing the company with advice, and what are its known strategies?

Ask others, too. What do they know about this company's strategy? What clues might the company be seeing that you are overlooking or misinterpreting? What does the company know about its reputation when it comes to discussing and doing M&A deals?

To whom can you talk who has been on your side of the table with this company in the past? What were that person's strategies throughout the steps in the process? If the deal closed, what happened to the startup afterward? Did the company follow through on what it said or did things take a different direction? If the deal didn't close, why? What fell apart?

Look beyond what the buying side is saying and look into what it is doing. How is the buyer valuing your company? Who is involved in this process and conversations and other communications (which can give you clues to the company's intent)?

If there is any talk about the future for your team, and whether the company plans to pay with cash or stock or financing, what does that tell you? What reactions have you had to any suggestions for integrating companies?

The bottom line is that understanding the buyer's strategy will illustrate how to show up in the best way and make this a no-brainer, must-do deal for the company.

Agreeing On the Meeting Location

Where should you meet buyers when it comes to the first real conversation on buying your business?

Your meeting location can be influential to the outcome of this meeting and getting to further meetings. What factors might you want to take into account before deciding on or agreeing to their request? How will your choices potentially affect your advantages and disadvantages and the outcomes?

Who Is Going to Be Part of the Meeting?

Who will be in this meeting? This may be a factor you have to take into consideration.

Which people will be there from your side of the table? Are they local to you? Are they even working in the same time zone? What will it cost you to have them there or at different locations?

If you are paying your attorney $500 an hour and your executives $200 an hour, and you are thinking about flying them out to Silicon Valley, NYC, or London for a long weekend for this meeting (the first of many), then that is going to add up pretty fast.

Make sure you aren't going to bankrupt yourself just talking about this deal or put yourself under so much financial strain that you end up having to sell the company for half as much.

If everyone participating in your deal is in the same city, then it can make a lot more financial and time sense to host the meeting on your home turf.

Of course, the other side may make the same arguments, too. It may come down to who needs to make the deal the most.

Home Games versus Intelligence Gathering

If money and time are no hurdle and are negligible to you, then the choice of where to meet may come down to where you see the best strategic advantage.

In sports, the home team is considered to have a significant home field advantage. So much so that specific rules have been created for many sports to make sure games are rotated, and important matches are held in neutral stadiums. In some cases, scoring rules may even be different.

The data seem to back this up. In the 2018–2019 premier league soccer season, 100 percent of Liverpool FC's losses were away matches. In the 2018–2019 NBA basketball season, the home team won the game 71 percent of the time. Away teams won only 29 percent of the time.

There are a variety of reasons the home field can provide an advantage. Many of them are psychological. Scientists have even discovered chemical and hormonal changes in athletes competing in a sporting event at home—more than regular training play.

Energy and routine can be a big part of it. Meeting on your home ground means you can sleep in your own bed, go through your own morning success ritual, and make sure you get a good cup of coffee. You'll be rested, in your zone, and on top of your game.

That isn't always the case if you are rushing to a meeting halfway around the world, you spent the night trying to sleep on a super-cramped Air France flight, and then had to hitchhike the last 25 miles on a camel after your rental car broke down in the desert.

At home, you also get to control everything about your environment. This is true for everything from the colors of the decor to the food and drinks, the temperature, lighting, presentation equipment, and availability of backups and tech support. You even have a say in the attitude of the people in the background and with whom your visitors interact. You can curate everything.

With all of that said, there can also be exclusive advantages to going to your acquirer's turf.

This offers some reconnaissance and intelligence gathering. It's a unique opportunity you may want to leverage as early in the deal as possible.

You'll be able to meet more of their team and the players in the process. You might get to peek inside the operation and see if it is really where you can see yourself and your team. You get to meet people in their natural habitat. This can show you far more than anything you can find online.

It is an opportunity to pick up all kinds of useful clues and data that can be used from the outset and throughout the negotiation process. You get to see how people are treated and how money is spent. The pictures on people's desks will tell you what is most important to them, and you might even end up at their homes after dinner. You can get great insight into their world view, influences, and perspectives.

In-Person versus Virtual Meetings

Although virtual meetings may give you less to work with, they can be far more efficient than flying around the world. They may lack the in-person connection, but you may have no choice. When possible, and the numbers make sense, meeting in person can offer real advantages.

However, if you aren't going to be involved personally later, or all future communication is going to be virtual anyway, then why not start virtually?

Virtual meetings don't mean you can slack on your preparation. Thorough preparation may be even more important in these scenarios. Be prepared mentally and be mentally present.

Have a good internet or phone connection and at least one or two backup connections and devices, as well as a second and third option, for where you will take the meeting. (The crazy technical difficulties only happen when you are trying to have a really important conversation.)

Whichever app you choose to use, having the ability to mute, pause, and share your screen is handy. Your choices range from Zoom to Google Meet, WhatsApp, Skype, and FaceTime.

Setting Up the Agenda for the Meeting

The meeting should have an agenda, and it should be tight.

Everyone at this meeting is busy, and their time is valuable. Keeping a tight time frame keeps the discussion focused and moving forward. It also avoids boredom.

In fact, you'll want to share as much as you feel comfortable with in advance of the meeting, as well as the set agenda, so that any real meeting time is spent being productive and moving the needle. If you get along well, you can always go out for drinks, dinner, or spend a few hours just getting to know each other and musing about future possibilities, if you really want to.

Keep your agenda short and simple:

- Introductions
- Buyer presentation

- Seller presentation
- Q&A session
- Recaps
- Laying down the next steps

Follow Up with Emails to Keep Them Warm

Hopefully you've walked out of this meeting with a commitment on the next step, and a deadline attached to it. It is probably a sign of weak salespersonship on your side, or a lack of interest and match on their side, if you don't.

Either way, it can pay to keep them warm, staying at the top of their mind, and keep things moving with follow-up emails. Don't be desperate, but be consistent.

Following are some great reasons to follow up:

- Providing access to additional data or requested information
- Updates on your company progress
- Thank-you emails for the meeting and time together
- Asking pertinent questions after consulting the rest of your advisors
- Announcing new developments or milestones your company is achieving
- Advising them of other interest in buying your company

Understanding How to Address Concerns

All experienced buyers should have questions, reservations, and concerns—at least if they've been in business long enough and have done a couple of these deals. If they don't, they may not be the type of acquirer you really want to put your company in the hands of.

Be sure to follow up as promised, with additional data and information.

If you feel they are taking a wait-and-see approach, don't expect them to be tracking your every move. Make some noise about your traction and send them a copy of the link to the news.

In other cases, they may not voice their concerns. One entrepreneur (who shall remain anonymous) didn't get an offer from Apple after their meeting. Later, Steve Jobs said they didn't think the seller would want to move out to California. The seller hadn't even asked. It's your job to anticipate concerns and objections and head them off proactively in your first meeting.

Questions Potential Acquirers May Ask You

When you show up to these meetings, you want to be as lined up as possible. The following sections explore the questions that you should be ready to answer.

Market

You have to be able to explain exactly how you fit in the existing and emerging market.

- How big is the market opportunity?
- What percentage of the market share do you hope to gain?
- Who is your best customer?
- How long will this take?
- What is your PR strategy?
- Who do you most aspire to be like?
- Who do you least want to be like?
- Why is this the right time for this product or service?
- What is your marketing strategy?

Traction

Acquirers will certainly want to know all about your current and expected success.

- How much feedback have you received so far?
- What changes have you made based on that feedback?
- How many actual users do you have?
- How long do users stay on average?
- How many actual sales have you made?
- What is the annual growth rate?
- What is your total rate of growth?
- Has growth been linear and consistent?
- What has held back your growth?
- Can you provide a demonstration of the product or service now?

Team

Naturally, acquirers will want to know all about your team.

- Where are your headquarters?
- Who are the founders?
- Who are the key team members?
- Do you have any existing board members?
- What key roles may need to be hired for soon?
- What experience do you have in this industry?
- What motivates you?
- Are there any other people who may claim they are owed or are responsible for your ideas?

Competition

Acquirers have a vested interest in understanding who your competitors are and what similarities and differences you share with them.

- Who are your competitors?
- What are your strengths and advantages over your competitors?

- What are your weaknesses or disadvantages?
- What barriers to entry or scale are there for you?
- Where is the competition letting down customers?
- Why haven't your competitors done this yet?
- How do your features differ?
- How do you compare on price?
- How do you compare on service?
- How do you compare on customer satisfaction?

Financials

You really should either know your financial information or have it quickly and easily available.

- How are you marketing your product or services?
- How much is your marketing budget?
- What are your per-customer acquisition costs?
- How much is your customer lifetime value?
- How much equity and debt have been raised in the past?
- Who participated in earlier rounds of fundraising?
- What is your burn rate?
- How long will it take to become profitable?
- What are the key metrics your team is focused on?
- What stock options have been given already?
- What is the distribution of equity?

Intellectual Property

One core area that acquirers are interested in is your intellectual property and all related legal and regulatory matters.

- What is unique about the company?
- What big problem does it solve?
- What legal risks do you see?

- Are you aware of any product liability risks?
- What regulatory risks could affect this business?
- What intellectual property do you own?
- Who developed any intellectual property owned?
- Have any employees or partners left who may challenge these rights?
- Are there any additional patents pending or planned?
- How are any current intellectual assets owned?

Business Model

Questions will come up about sales, marketing, customers, and all aspects of your business model.

- Which specific marketing channels are you using?
- Why are you using these marketing channels?
- What is your plan B if these sales channels are interrupted?
- What profit margins are you operating on?
- How will scaling impact profit margins?
- What pivots have you already made?
- Can you tell me a story about how a customer decided to choose you and their experience with your product?
- Who in this organization is most replaceable?
- What unique features are you working on?
- What other streams of revenue can be added to this?

Corporate Structure

Similar to knowing your team, understanding your corporate culture helps acquirers truly understand what makes your organization tick.

- How is the company currently organized?
- Who holds which titles?

- How are shares split?
- Is there an existing board or advisors?
- Where is the company registered?
- Who handles accounting?
- What unique skills and talents does each owner contribute?
- Name someone you chose not to include as a founder—and why?
- Who filed the company?
- Who is the registered agent on record?

Existing M&A Process

You also have to be able to explain everything about the mergers and acquisitions process.

- What is your exit goal?
- What is your expected time frame for this?
- What is the valuation of the company?
- How are you determining the current valuation?
- How do you see your integration with our company?

11

Getting to a Letter of Intent (LOI)

YOU'VE DONE THE PREP WORK, and you've presented and met with potential buyers. Now, you hope to field letters of intent (LOIs) from interested acquirers.

A letter of intent is an important step in the right direction when you're looking to sell your company and achieve an exit. But there are a variety of misconceptions about LOIs in the M&A space. So what are the most important points of the document? What do you need to know—and do—before moving forward?

In essence, an LOI is a document expressing an interest in moving to the next stage of pursuing an acquisition of your company.

An LOI is a stronger document than an IOI (indication of interest). The IOI is more like someone raising his or her hand or cold emailing you and stating that he or she might be interested in buying your company for a rough estimate or within a rough price range. The buyer probably hasn't done much homework, but if you're interested, then the person will be interested in snooping around a little more to see if it is a match. It helps the company streamline its workload, and it'll proceed only if there is a seller already interested in making a deal at an attractive price.

An IOI may come before an LOI in startup M&A, but it is not necessarily a precursor to moving into making a deal.

An LOI is not an entity or asset purchase agreement, either. These agreements are the actual legal contract that will be used to close the transaction, spelling out all of the tiny details and adjustment calculations that determine the final figures and that govern what happens in the months and years after the deal is finalized. That means escrows, warranties, employment contracts, and ongoing capitalization, resources, and performance metrics for your business in a merger, and more. This voluminous document can clearly take a lot longer to formulate, negotiate, vote on, get approved, and acquire all of the necessary signatures.

The LOI is an interim document that fills this time gap and links the buyer and you as seller together in the meantime. It also helps you both feel a lot better about sharing information and investing any more time and money working on the potential transaction.

Why an LOI Is So Important

An LOI is the first real tangible indication that a buyer may be serious and has three main roles:

1. To lay out the rough nature and terms of the deal
2. To identify key points and points that need to be fleshed out before closing
3. To protect the parties involved in the process

Sharing M&A offers and potential deals with your teams, shareholders, and others carries a significant amount of risk in itself, so you want to be sure the buyer is serious and committed.

Obviously, sharing data and internal information and opening certain lines of communication with outside companies and third parties bring even more tangible risks—especially when some of them may be direct competitors or soon could be if they buy another startup in your space or decide to try to replicate your success themselves. So the LOI in an M&A situation helps protect you and minimizes your risk of loss should the deal not come to completion or the buyer and its representatives prove not to be acting in good faith.

A real LOI in this situation also lays out the general proposed terms of the offer. It is not final or binding. You can expect terms to change and be adjusted and generally not in your favor. Similar to a term sheet in fundraising mode, this document also helps to ensure that you are at least in the right ballpark in terms of price and deal structure. You do not want to waste time with a buyer who is not going to meet you where you need to be.

It should suffice to say that you do not want to jump deep into talks, share sensitive data, or discuss the costs associated without a closely aligned LOI.

Breaking Down the LOI

LOIs have a letter format and can vary in length. They can be vague or in-depth. This often depends on the size of the deal, the buyer, and how the transaction will be structured. What you negotiate as the seller is also a factor.

Following are the main sections or provisions that will be covered in most LOIs, which you should definitely go over with your corporate lawyer.

Who

The LOI begins with a customary formal introduction of the buyer or offeror and the target company.

Overview of the Transaction

This section lays out the desired or anticipated structure and initial top-line numbers. Will it be a cash or stock deal or a mixture of both? What is the gross purchase price or amount of stock the buyer expects to pay before adjustments? Will performance-based compensation be included? What are the proposed time lines for additional payments or disbursements after closing?

Due Diligence

Most often, the LOI will contain highly generic information about the due diligence the offer is subject to. It will include all customary verifications and validations of your claims and their investment thesis, including regulations, taxes, accounting, and so on.

Confidentiality

A legal confidentiality and nondisclosure agreement should be attached and referenced as an exhibit to the LOI. This separate legal document should detail the consequences and legal jurisdiction for any breach of confidentiality or improper use or disclosure of information obtained during talks and during the due diligence period. The information may be included as one of only two legally binding clauses in an M&A letter of intent. Note that both parties will be legally bound by this agreement and any other documents that they sign.

The Exclusivity Period

Expect the LOI to also include a requested exclusivity period and possible separate exclusivity agreement. This is the second legally binding document you may sign as part of this stage of the M&A process.

A 60- to 90-day exclusivity period is not uncommon. It may be even longer during challenging economic times, as well as during larger and more complex deals when approvals from regulators are sure to take longer. There may be provisions for an extension as well.

During this exclusivity period, you, as the seller, will be legally bound not to take other incoming bids. You will also not be allowed to shop your company.

Comparing Valuations

This is a good time to talk to your prospective buyer about how the company is valuing your business. What is it that the company really wants to buy, and why? Then, how are the buyers coming up with their price?

What is the formula or method being used for valuation? This is important to know. This information can help you gauge and foresee any fluctuations in price or payout based on these calculations. If their stock price changes, how will that change the deal? If your income goes down during the due diligence period, what is that likely to mean for the price? What if certain tax rules change before the deal is closed? This information can also help you keep your business optimized for the most important metrics for your buyer over the months ahead. (As an example, the buyer may not care about revenues, but the team wants to see active user counts growing fast.)

Measuring Suitability of the Potential Buyer

We've already covered filtering and searching for target buyers. We've gone over the ins and outs of financial and strategic buyers. We've also covered looking for positive indicators and red flag indicators in buyers through the M&A process. But at this point, it's wise to step back and assess the suitability of the buyer, *before* signing an LOI and launching forward.

Here are four key questions to ask when evaluating the feasibility of a buyer that has approached you with an LOI.

Can the Company Buy You?

Does this company really have the financial strength to buy you and keep your company going, if that is part of the arrangement? What factors between receiving the LOI and closing the deal may affect that ability? What about macroeconomic factors? Access to capital markets and financing? Is there anything that could substantially affect the stock price and market cap? What about regulatory issues?

Will the Company Buy You?

How likely is it that the company will really follow through on this offer or at least something close to it? How much do you trust the buyer? Does the company have a track record of successfully closing mergers and acquisitions or is this its first attempt? Are there any potential personal clashes between your shareholders or key team members and the company's executives that could derail the deal?

How much due diligence has the company done? If the buyer hasn't really dug in to get a good handle on your company, then there are countless excuses for the buyer to back out or keep dropping the price and renegotiating terms. The more due diligence the company has done up front, the less risk of the deal falling apart. You may want to encourage the company to do as much as possible (without giving up secure and sensitive data) in advance of going to an LOI.

What Will It Be Like?

What will the process of going through the M&A process be like? What will being merged and owned by this buyer be like?

Will it be enjoyable, inspiring, and empowering? Or is it going to be a living hell every single day for the next few years, followed by years of regretting the deal and its ramifications for customers and the world?

It might seem hard to determine on the surface, but you'll get a great feel for all this in your meeting with the current CEO. You can examine the company culture and fit to yours, check out the corporate reputation as an employer, and test out teams working together.

Even better, be sure to talk to other founders who have engaged in M&A talks and transactions with this buyer before—both those who were acquired and those who saw their deals fall apart before closing. What do they have to say? What tips can they offer?

How Does It Compare?

How does this buyer compare to others? How does this buyer compare to your ideal buyer choices? Not just in relation to price or terms, but for the future of your venture, the mission, process, and real match in synergies?

Hostile versus Friendly Buyers

Most entrepreneurs do not think this far ahead. Some offers and processes will be friendly, and others may be hostile. If there are inbound offers that you know will be bad for the mission, your team, customers, and your company, then there are steps you can take.

Preempting hostile takeover bids can be done through "shark-repellent" strategies that make your company unattractive to potential buyers in advance. Of course, any experienced investors you bring into your cap table who are purely focused on a financial exit may not approve these measures.

Other tactics can be used later to turn off hostile buyers from making offers. These scorched earth or poison pill strategies are designed to sabotage hostile offers. They can include defensive mergers with allies, selling off key assets, or high amounts of debt leverage at excruciatingly high interest rates.

Be aware that these strategies can also be counterproductive and self-sabotaging. You may avoid being acquired, but if you get it wrong, you could find yourself bankrupt with no appealing potential exits.

Be sure to speak with your lawyers about these issues and strategies before doing anything so that you know what's legally permissible and the liabilities of any potential approaches.

Considerations before Signing

It bears repeating that although LOIs are mostly nonbinding, they typically have provisions, clauses, and attached documents that are legally binding on you as the seller. An LOI is a step in the process of getting to a real purchase agreement, and will keep the deal moving as you work through a more detailed draft and finer negotiations. *Make sure you are happy and confident in the LOI before you sign.* It probably isn't going to get better or move further in your favor during the due diligence period.

In fact, although it is in the buyer's best interest to be as vague and brief as possible in the LOI, it is in your interest as the seller to make sure to glean as much detail as possible from the document. Negotiate as much as you can up front. Otherwise, the buyer will claim all of the clauses are standard. The company will want you to give up other trade-offs to get assurances or different basics you want—including everything from earnouts to employee compensation packages. Ask about how financial adjustments will be made here.

Whether you really trust the company with your data and secret sauce may come down to gut instinct. Don't ignore what your instincts tell you.

Understand your go-shop and no-shop clauses. Will you be required to solicit other bids and offers for your company? Or will you be prohibited from shopping around, auctioning, or entertaining talks and offers from other buyers, which may even be far better than the one you have now?

What happens if you sign, and then the buyer just pulls out? How much is this buyer willing to put into escrow to show that the company is really serious and committed? How much of that can you get your hands on as a breach or breakup fee to compensate you for lost time, expenses, and confidentiality?

The LOI Template

Below is a good example of an LOI. Note this is just an example, and you will need to consult with your corporate lawyer.

[Buyer]

[Seller]

Acquisition Loi

This Letter of Intent (this "LOI"), dated as of [ ], confirms that [buyer] ("name" or the "Buyer") is interested in acquiring all or substantially all of the business, assets, or equity securities of [seller] ("name" or the "Seller").

In this LOI, the Buyer's possible acquisition of Seller's business, assets, or equity securities is referred to as the "Acquisition." The parties wish to commence negotiating a definitive written acquisition agreement providing for the Acquisition (a "Definitive Agreement"). To facilitate the negotiation of a Definitive Agreement, Buyer has prepared this LOI. The execution of a Definitive Agreement would be subject to the satisfactory completion of Buyer's ongoing due diligence investigation of the Seller's business and would also be subject to approval by the Buyer's Board of Directors.

The provisions of this Term Sheet are intended only as an expression of interest on behalf of the Buyer, are not intended to be legally binding on any party or the Seller, and are expressly subject to the negotiation and execution of an appropriate Definitive Agreement. In addition, nothing in this LOI should be construed as an offer or commitment on the part of Buyer to submit a definitive proposal.

(*continued*)

(*continued*)

Based on the information currently known to Buyer, it is proposed that a Definitive Agreement would include the following terms:

Seller:	
Buyer:	
Authority:	The Seller and the Buyer have full authority, subject to the provisions of this LOI, to enter into these negotiations regarding this proposed transaction and to execute this LOI.
Structure of Transaction:	To be determined following business and legal due diligence
Purchase Price:	
Payment Terms:	
Miscellaneous:	
Closing Date:	[ ]

The parties intend to be bound by the following provisions:

Confidentiality:	The parties agree that the existence and content of this LOI shall be Confidential Information, as defined in that certain Mutual Nondisclosure Agreement, dated as of [ ] by and between [buyer] and [seller] (the "NDA"), except that this Term Sheet's existence and content may be revealed to the parties' respective boards of directors, legal advisers, financial advisors, and senior management.

Exclusivity:	For a period of [ ] days following the execution of the LOI, the Seller will not, directly or indirectly, through any representative or otherwise, solicit or entertain offers from, negotiate with, or in any manner encourage, discuss, accept, or consider any proposal of any other person relating to the purchase of any assets or capital stock or any business unit of [seller], in whole or in part, whether directly or indirectly, through purchase, merger, consolidation, or otherwise. The Seller will immediately notify Buyer regarding any contact between Seller, or their respective representatives, and any other person regarding any such offer or proposal or any related inquiry, and if made in writing, furnish a copy thereof.
Due Diligence:	Subject to the NDA, each party shall use commercially reasonable efforts to deliver to the other party a complete set of due diligence materials as reasonably requested by the other party and as mutually agreed on by the parties within [ ] days after the date of this LOI.
Costs:	Buyer and each Seller will be responsible for and bear all of its respective costs and expenses (including any broker's or finder's fees and the expenses of their representatives) incurred at any time in connection with pursuing or consummating the Acquisition.
Modification:	The LOI may be amended, supplemented, or otherwise modified by a writing executed by the parties.

(*continued*)

(*continued*)

Governing Law:	All matters relating to or arising out of this LOI will be governed by and construed under the laws of [ ], without regard to conflicts of law principles that would require the application of any other law.
Termination:	Unless agreed to by the Buyer as evidenced in a separate writing, the proposed terms of this Term Sheet shall no longer be applicable after the close of business on [ ]; provided, however, that the NDA, in accordance with its terms, shall survive any termination of this LOI. Either party may terminate this LOI by written notice served to the other party before the close of business on [ ] or if extended by the Buyer, before execution by the Seller of a Definitive Agreement.

This term sheet is agreed in accordance with the terms and conditions set forth above by the parties set forth below on [ ].

Agreed:

Seller:

[name]

[title]

[seller]

Buyer:

[name]

[title]

[buyer]

12

Communication with Stakeholders

COMMUNICATING WITH STAKEHOLDERS IS CRITICAL throughout the M&A process. Understanding to whom you need to talk and what their roles are is critical to the success of the deal. It can greatly affect the net outcome, how smoothly the transaction goes (or not), and the legal and financial risks you may incur by not following protocols.

There can be a variety of stakeholders involved in this process. Know who they are, what their roles are, and how to interact with them.

The Role of the Board of Directors

What is the role of the board of directors in an M&A transaction?

As the founder or CEO, you may end up getting the first real call, conversation, or pitch to sell your company. Despite your history with the company, it is important that you don't forget your new place in the organization.

When it comes to corporate law, most jurisdictions dictate that the executive team operates under the direction of the board. The board of directors governs. They decide the strategy and direction of the company. The management team, including the CEO, COO, CFO, and CIO, operates under their guidance and simply executes on their decisions.

That means you don't really get to have an opinion on an offer or price. By law, you are operating at the direction and on the decisions of the board. Otherwise, it wouldn't be much different than your CMO or customer service lead engaging in an M&A conversation with a larger competitor.

This can be a hard pill to swallow at first. It is hard to get your head around as a first time entrepreneur and founder who just threw yourself into this business, and all of a sudden you have investors, shareholders, and a board of directors.

It will make a lot more sense your second time around, when you are approaching building your organization more strategically, with the end in mind from the beginning.

Of course, in turn, the board of directors is serving at the pleasure of the shareholders with voting rights.

Typically, and depending on the jurisdiction governing the corporation, the approval of a merger or acquisition will require the unanimous approval of the board of directors or the majority of voting shareholders. The majority of votes may be differentiated by the majority of all voting shares, the majority of shares of each class, or the majority of votes at the meeting. (Another good reason for founders to create and hold super voting rights.)

This all applies to the buy side of the table as well.

In many cases, early-stage startups and their boards haven't yet developed a formal M&A or exit strategy and policies for it. This is something that will come along with a more mature company, one that is also making acquisitions of its own.

When it comes to making decisions, and especially M&A, the board of directors is governed by two implicit rules and protocols:

- Duty of loyalty
- Duty of care

Directors have a fiduciary duty of loyalty to the company. This means operating in the company's best interest. It involves taking action and making deals, ensuring privacy, and protecting confidentiality. Although many founders may interpret "loyalty to the company" as the mission and founding vision and values, it is the other shareholders who are going to sue if they don't love the decisions made. So it really often comes down to a duty to the shareholders' desires and interests.

Then there is the duty of care. That means putting enough due care into ensuring that a proper acquisition process is carried out. It all comes down to due diligence. Your acquirer's thorough due diligence can seem like a real pain and overkill, but it is fulfilling their legal obligation to their company and shareholders.

During M&A discussions and transactions, the board has several special roles and jobs. If anything, the board members must go above and beyond to demonstrate and prove they are adhering to these two legal duties.

Weighing All Options

The board must weigh all potential options before accepting an offer in the form of an LOI, even if it is a great one. Options may include going public or raising new rounds of funding and remaining independent. It can also mean shopping around and soliciting other bids to ensure maximization of the price and returns for investors and shareholders.

Guiding Valuation and Fit

The board should be involved in data-driven discussions on value and strategic fit. It is their job to set value expectations based on facts. They should understand the danger of high valuations with little rationale, how shaky that can make deals, and the problems it can cause internally when other shareholders start thinking too big.

In addition, be sure that shareholders don't sabotage a great deal because they are trying to hold out for too much money or have an unrealistic view of the value. At the same time, board members are also responsible for making sure the valuation of the company and any assets sold are not so overvalued that it could be considered fraud in the future.

After the closing, down the road, if the acquirer gets into financial trouble, or has trouble repaying any loans the company used to finance the deal, the buyer is going to claim there was fraud in the overvaluation of what the company paid for.

Being the Voice of Objectivity

Management, and especially founders, are subject to unconscious bias. They are on the frontlines and in the trenches. They have lived with an extreme level of passion and optimism. They are also subject to the deepest swings in doubt and panic in a crisis. They may have the least experience at the big-picture level. They are much more likely to act emotionally rather than objectively, and that can be risky financially and legally. The board is there to temper these elements with their experience and wisdom.

On top of that, the board members need to prove their own objectivity in the process. This typically means forming special committees to evaluate and oversee this process, and outsourcing things such as valuation opinions to third parties who are able to think, research, and present objectively.

Post-merger Integration

Experienced board members can bring a lot to the table when it comes to post-merger integration, and the strategy and tactics leading up to the closing that will determine how well the two companies will integrate.

Board members may also continue to play a role after the merger or acquisition. Harvard released a study[1] on Fortune 500–level companies that stated that board members on the acquiring side stay on after the deal 83 percent of the time. Directors on the sell side stay on 34 percent of the time, and just 29 percent of external directors end up continuing with the company.

Keeping Investors Updated in the M&A Process

Investors can have a lot of sway in the M&A process, especially those who have put in a lot of money and have been given significant amounts of equity.

Most institutional investors will already have a seat on your board as part of the terms of their investment. They'll be among the first alerted to talks of a deal.

Eventually, all may have a vote. If you've chosen your investors well and your visions and time lines have remained aligned, you ought to be in agreement on handling any offers or selling the company. They should want what is best for the company, and if that is selling, then they should be on board.

Of course, they are also in the investment business. They invested with the expectation and hope of a certain level of return. Perhaps most important, they have an obligation to deliver on the returns they promised their limited partners.

They are going to be looking at the earnings multiples they will get back with this exit. In most cases, they will have negotiated multiples and preferences that will ensure they get paid first and best in the transaction.

In fact, when you agree to take their money, at least from professional angels and venture capitalists, you are really committing to delivering an exit for them. Of course, there can be disagreements and differences of opinion when it comes to selling—especially

[1] https://corpgov.law.harvard.edu/2015/09/07/role-of-the-board-in-ma/

about the right time and price. Some may want to hold out for more. Private equity and strategic corporate investors may not want you to sell out, particularly if they view it as potentially detrimental to their own businesses.

When investors may not be part of the board, it pays to be prepared. It pays to be able to present well, to include the other options, and to prepare for potential future tangents, valuations, and the pros and cons of selling. There's also the question "Why now?" (or "Why not now?"). There's also the matter of which options best match what they signed up for or provide the best future, given the reality of the current situation and outlook.

Then, keep them appropriately updated on developments and upcoming votes. This may be by phone or email. Just make sure you keep information contained that you are required to keep confidential. Experienced investors will know the roller coaster and circus of going through an M&A deal. They will want to be looped in, but they should be able to handle the uncertainty more than you are prepared for.

The Dos and Don'ts with Employees

Telling employees about offers and potential sales can be one of the major deal killers in M&A.

First, you can't control confidential information when you broadcast it across your organization. Second, although you want to be fully transparent with your team members, you can seriously jeopardize your whole business by leaking information prematurely.

You can throw their whole world into chaos. Once they start Googling terms about mergers and acquisitions, they'll mostly find information that makes them panic and become defensive. They'll feel they need to be proactive about securing another job or fighting for their stock options or benefits. Doing a good job at their daily tasks can quickly become the last thing on their minds, through no fault of their own. That can not only derail the deal but also be disastrous for the business you are left with when it falls apart.

As much as you love and trust them and want them to be there with you through the process, and to enjoy a great outcome, most advice about this is to wait as long as possible to tell most of your employees.

When it comes time to tell them, be transparent. Explain why this is the best move for the company and the benefits for them. Get their buy-in so that they will continue to help you power through.

13

Negotiating the Price Tag

You've met with potential acquirers, received an LOI, and have communicated it to your board members. Now comes your chance to negotiate and maximize the value of the deal. So, what are the most important elements here? How do you make sure you are getting the best deal you possibly can, without being too greedy and turning away great buyers?

Price versus Terms

The price tag may have value for a couple of reasons—like crossing the mental barrier (for some of your investors or acquirers) and perhaps establishing your credibility and reputation for launching future ventures. Having sold a company for $1 billion or more certainly carries some weight. Many significant acquirers won't do small deals. They are more likely to buy roll-ups with higher price tags. A big price tag can make investors and cofounders feel special and accomplished.

Although the top line price tag shouldn't be completely dismissed, the terms are far more important because they may dictate these outcomes:

- How you get paid in terms of currency and when
- Who gets how much
- The structure and net after taxes (which can make all the difference)
- How enjoyable or demoralizing the process is
- How good the deal really is for the company, mission, and customers after the transaction.

Be keenly aware that giving up a lower top line price may actually be more beneficial when it comes to the net proceeds and future (thanks to the terms) and that a higher price tag may not always yield a better outcome.

The terms (and, more specifically, what the outcomes will mean for you and all the others involved) are far more important than the price or valuation.

Communicating Outcomes

There are two parts to communicating outcomes:

- Communicating the outcomes of different offers to your stakeholders
- Communicating needed outcomes for your shareholders and the company to your potential buyer

Your board, shareholders, and cofounders need to know what different potential offers really mean to them. A $1 billion offer may sound great, but it could still net, for some of those involved, zero dollars—or they may have to make further long-term commitments in order to get paid anything.

Is this a last chance deal for some of your investors just to get their capital back? Or can they expect the 10× returns they were hoping for?

Of course, you hope you all are on the same page as to what is really best for the company going forward. After all, that is the real mission and obligation.

When it comes to communicating outcomes with interested buyers, you should be clear about the necessary outcomes that will make or break a deal:

- A minimum desired return to your investors
- A specific minimum you'll get to walk away with
- Provisions that will guarantee your company continues to survive and thrive

Obviously, there are expectations for these asks or musts, too.

Some companies will find themselves in a crisis situation, in which selling is the most attractive option. If it is a matter of selling, going bankrupt, or folding the company, then you have to take what you can get. You can and should still try to negotiate the best deals, though you may not have the ability to demand much.

In other cases, your startup may have hit a ceiling or maybe you've just lost interest. It may be most efficient to grow your venture by merging or putting it in the hands of a much larger corporation. Perhaps, you just want to be set free to explore another venture that is consuming your thoughts and interest. In these situations, price may be a distant second or third to the terms and speed of exiting.

Pushing for a Deadline

Deadlines can be hugely important when it comes to M&A deals.

You should have deadlines on offers, be wrapping up negotiations and inking a purchase agreement, and closing the deal.

Drawn-out negotiations can be a downward spiral. Even if the market improves and your company performance increases and the tangible value of the company goes up, you are probably going to find it hard to renegotiate a much higher price mid-process. That means trying to find a way to back out without legal liability and starting all over again or leaving a lot of money on the table.

More likely, you could face a declining market, business disruptions, and running low on cash—all of which make it likely your acquirer will want to renegotiate a much lower price to account for any loss in value and increased risk.

If you are close to alignment in negotiations on price, don't let it get drawn out too long. If you are making counter offers, put a deadline on it. Make them sign or move on.

The same goes for closing the deal. Some M&A deals may close in just a few weeks. Most take months. Some can even take a year or more to get to closing and funding. Final payments from earnouts and other terms may not come for years after the close.

The further out the closing is, the more risk. The more time that goes by, the higher the risk that the buyer will back out of the deal. That may be due to a change in management, strategy, its financial position, or disruption in wider markets, as well as declines in your own company or the urgency to buy it. If the company wants out, it will find a way, even if it takes a hellish due diligence experience to get you to walk away and pull the plug.

Time means internal risk as well. It is more time you are tied up dealing with this deal, rather than working on the business and pushing growth or seizing the perfect timing for the next venture you hope to pursue. As the excitement wears off, your team and shareholders may also lose interest in the deal or think there are better options. Some could sabotage it and cost the company and other stakeholders a lot in the process. That risk keeps growing over time.

Increasing Price with a Bidding War

You owe it yourself and your shareholders to get the maximum value for your startup. You can't know that you are getting that or prove it to others or in court unless you've solicited other bids for your company.

Bidding wars are a fantastic, proven tool for maximizing offer prices. It's why auctions have been popular for hundreds of years. Bidding is what big startups such as eBay were built on, as well as iconic brands such as Sotheby's.

Once you've received an offer in the form of an LOI that you are taking seriously, you really have the obligation to shop around. You may do that as a company yourself by putting together your pitch-book and presenting the opportunity for other target buyers to make an offer before it is too late and they miss out. Or you can hire an investment banker to handle this part and drum up a bidding war for your company.

It is basic Psychology 101. People can't help but be motivated in bidding war scenarios. The competition drives them, as does the fear of missing out. Provided there is a fundamental need and desire to buy your company, with a good story about the future value, they can justify that to their investors, and there's a good chance you can push up the price.

Even if your initial offer came from what you see as the best buyer, the process and competition can drive the buyer to up its bid or even just speed up the process and agree to a shorter closing period, with more attractive terms for your side of the table.

Again, don't be too overconfident or greedy to the point that you lose the initial offer and fail to sell or burn exit opportunities with these buyers in the future. Set yourself an internal deadline, too.

Maximizing Value on the Buyer and Seller Sides

Warren Buffett says, "Price is what you pay, value is what you get."

How do you elevate and maximize the value of this deal for both your company and shareholders, as well as your buyers?

Price and value may be related, but they aren't always directly intertwined with each other every step of the way. There are different forms of value for both sides, some of which can be independent of the price.

Although "win-win" may sound cliche these days, both sides do have to feel like they are winning something. Otherwise, they aren't going to stick with the deal—especially not in a transaction like this, which can be long and full of challenges and excuses to back out.

What can you do to increase the value of the deal for your side of the table?

One thing that may seem important—and pivotal—from some board members, cofounders, and key team members with equity is what happens to them after the close. This may be purely psychological and ego-driven or there may be income and a career path in mind. Securing their positions in the company after a merger, plus good job titles, compensation packages, and learning opportunities, can provide them with lots of perceived value and may not really cost your acquirer anything extra.

Earnouts and other post-closing, performance-based payouts can also boost value for your side. This greatly de-risks this portion of capital invested by a buyer. In fact, anything you can do to lower and remove risk for your buyer will make a big difference. Not having to factor in that extra liability or potential for loss raises the value of every penny the buyer puts in. That can justify a higher price for your company, too.

Another way to provide confidence and reduce risk for the buyer is through contracts. Contracts, such as for sales and revenues with customers, suppliers, distributors, and even property leases, provide security going forward. Anything that locks in income and keeps costs fixed helps.

Given that failed integration is typically the main source of loss and failure in these transactions, the better you can prove integration can be done well, the more value you are creating. Test, test, test. Put teams together and run collaborative campaigns together. And if you can exceed expectations, that can add a lot of dollars to both sides.

Taxes make all the difference between the gross top line and the net value. Anything you can do in preparing your finances and structuring the deal in a more tax-savvy way can add a lot of value for everyone, even without any changes to the price. It matters for the taxes they are exposed to and what bite gets taken out of your investors' payouts.

If you know your buyer as well as you should, then you should have a clear understanding of what the buyer wants, what the buyer is really trying to acquire, and what has value to the buyer. Many of your other assets may not be of interest to the buyer. In fact, such assets may be considered a hassle and costly to manage and liquidate. You can help the buyer create more value, while retaining more value on your side. This may include IP, real estate assets, equipment, and more, such as items you can use to start a new business or sell off to create more cash proceeds.

Thinking Like a Buyer

Successful negotiations are all about being able to put yourself into the mind of the buyer and being able to structure a deal that gives them their musts. This checks the most important boxes for you, too.

Give and Take

Unfortunately, just throwing out your best offer first, even if it is a good one for them, doesn't always work. They want to feel like they are winning something and getting a deal, just as people on your side of the table expect.

By knowing a buyer's triggers and levers and your essential shortlist, you can create a give-and-take scenario in which you appear to concede on the things the buyer wants in exchange for getting more of what you want (for example, your closing time frame and price in exchange for accepting its preferred method of payment and other small technical concessions).

Price Thresholds

In some cases, buyers feel better being just under a certain price point. Maybe $880 million makes them feel a whole lot better than paying $1 billion; yet, the details may make it more profitable for you. Or paying $2 billion may actually do more for their ego and reputation, even if they are overpaying—like being the first to buy a $100 million NYC penthouse. The bragging rights and press may be worth the splurge for a few fund managers and tech companies.

Appearing Smart

People want to look smart in front of their peers. They want to be admired by people for their intelligence.

As already discussed, the more you can de-risk this deal for them, the better. Beyond the money, it gives them the confidence they won't look foolish if the outcome implodes on them.

If you can convince them they are seeing the opportunity before others or they are seeing it for its real, higher value, that can also be a draw for those looking to make their mark.

Paranoia

Although you may do better just focusing on your own business, many subscribe to the mindset that others are out there plotting their downfall, working teams overtime to take them out of the game. They are paranoid about their competition and about being beaten out and overtaken, often rightly so. In this scenario, price should take a back seat compared to timing, getting the deal, and locking up your company before their competition does (and then uses it against them).

Where Is the Value for the Buyer?

What is it that your buyer is really trying to acquire? Is it your IP, data, customers, team, income streams and yields, or something else? Use this knowledge to maximize the exit for your company and shareholders. Know this information and assign most of the price and negotiations there. Kindly be willing to exclude other elements the buyer doesn't care about, and consider other ways to get value out of those.

Will You Move?

Ironically, Big Tech and Silicon Valley are still very local and about physical presence, despite the fact they are supposedly driving so many virtual and cloud-based innovations. If you are willing to relocate and be under their physical umbrella, then use that as a bargaining chip or bonus you can offer. Make sure you offer it, because the buyer won't always ask. They often just assume.

14

The Due Diligence Stage

THERE IS NO GENTLE WAY to say it: Due diligence is hell.

By this point, you've come a long way. Yet, there is still a distance to go in this process, and the due diligence stage can be one of the longest phases—and the most grueling.

If you are fortunate, you may be one of the few who sees this time blaze by in a few weeks, and you could be moving on to a whole new phase before you realize it. In other cases, this period can be drawn out for many months or even a year or more. Hopefully, you'll land somewhere less than that.

If you thought due diligence for fundraising was a pain, or if you thought it was a lot of work shopping your business around finding a great potential buyer and negotiating the terms, then get ready for that pain and work on a whole new level.

For those who have gone through the process of getting a mortgage to buy a house, it isn't too different in workload and theory. At first, you are consumed with finding the right home to buy. Once you think you've nailed that, you have all of the back-and-forth negotiations. Then, you finally get an offer accepted.

But instead of being able to finally breathe and relax, the real work is just beginning. Due diligence is necessary to validate and prove everything required and be certain that the value of the collateral is there. This can lead to last-minute glitches, delays, and renegotiations. Before the closing happens, there can be a lot of sleepless nights and stress.

This experience can be quite a shock for those not anticipating it. It is far more stressful than you imagine. Expect it to be really hard. Anything less will feel really good.

Beat the grueling toll this could have on you mentally and physically by preparing yourself in advance. Make sure the team members involved are also clued in and prepared for what to expect and that they can deal with it well.

Putting Together the Deal Room

Your deal room can make or break the deal, and it will certainly greatly affect how quickly you can close the deal (or not close it). It also has the ability to substantially affect the terms and price of the deal.

Physical versus Virtual Deal Rooms

For the most part, physical deal rooms (also known as *data rooms*) have become redundant. The status quo used to be a dedicated physical room for physical document storage, with restricted access (only for those with permission to view them).

Of course, physical rooms full of physical paper just aren't practical any more. It certainly isn't efficient. The exception may be for government-involved deals, where extra security is paramount.

Today, virtual deal rooms (VDRs) are much more common and expected, especially with the globalization of business.

Here are the benefits of VDRs:

- Saving enormous amounts of pollution and trees
- More efficient and profitable to use, saving time and money

- Greater speed in uploading requested documents and pushing the deal forward
- Clarity in collaboration, with Q&A and note-leaving ability
- Easy searching and location of documents
- Ease of cross-referencing and linking data
- Clear tracking of all information and records of who has viewed what
- Secure storage of data in the cloud, with no paper to be lost or stolen

Deal Room Software

A wide range of deal room software is currently available. Some of the popular options include Merrill, Intralinks, Venue, ShareFile, Mixado, Digify, Firmex, DealVDR, ShareVault, and DealRoom. These are not recommendations or endorsements—this is simply a sampling of options to explore.

Instead of using dedicated deal room providers, you can always place the documents into a folder and share them via Google Drive or Dropbox.

If you want to explore deal room software options, look for these things in M&A deal room software:

- High-level cybersecurity
- The option to revoke access and permissions at any time
- Ability to track views and who accessed what and when
- View-only permissions
- Differing levels of access for different roles
- No long contracts

Who Should Have Access to Your VDR?

When you create your virtual deal room, you need to consider who has access to it. There are a lot of people who shouldn't be able to access it. You probably don't want your entire staff, clients, customers, the press, the general public, or any parties not involved in the deal to be able to access your VDR. People you might want to grant permission to your VDR may include the following:

- Cofounders
- Executive management
- Lawyers
- Investment bankers
- Deal leads and committee members
- Post-closing integration leads
- Team members responsible for loading data to the deal room

What Information Should Be Uploaded to Your Deal Room?

A lot of people are uncertain of what information to provide in their deal room. Although the nature of your deal might influence some of the specifics, it is important to consider all of the potentially relevant options. Identifying, preparing, and uploading the information can be a lot of work, but the effort is necessary and pays off in the end. Following are the categories of information that you should consider:

1. Organization
   - ☐ 1.01 Certificate of incorporation (or equivalent) and all amendments and restatements
   - ☐ 1.02 By-laws (or equivalent), as currently in effect
   - ☐ 1.03 List of all business names used by or registered for use by the Company
   - ☐ 1.04 List of any and all subsidiaries and affiliates of the Company and jurisdiction of formation
   - ☐ 1.05 List of all jurisdictions in which the Company owns or leases (either as lessor or lessee) assets or has done so since incorporation

- ☐ 1.06 List of all jurisdictions in which the Company is qualified as a foreign entity, has applied for such qualification, or has substantial contacts
- ☐ 1.07 Minutes, including minutes of meetings of the board of directors, board committees, or the shareholders (or any equivalents); written consents of any of the foregoing in lieu of a meeting; and all materials distributed to the board, board committees, and the shareholders (or any equivalents) at any meeting
- ☐ 1.08 List of any business acquisitions or dispositions made by the Company
- ☐ 1.09 List of all persons who have been or who currently are officers or directors (or equivalent)

2. Capitalization and Securityholders
   - ☐ 2.01 List of Company securities authorized and outstanding that indicates the holders, amounts, and classes or series of such securities and copies of securities transfer books and stock ledgers
   - ☐ 2.02 Agreements to issue and/or register securities
   - ☐ 2.03 Agreements relating to voting of securities, preemptive rights, restrictions on transfers, rights of first refusal, and any other grants of rights in respect of the Company's securities
   - ☐ 2.04 All warrants, options, or other agreements relating to rights to acquire securities of the Company or requiring the issuance and/or registration of such securities
   - ☐ 2.05 All plans and grant or award documents for any stock option, stock bonus, stock purchase, or other equity-based compensatory programs for employees, consultants, advisors, and/or directors (or equivalent)
   - ☐ 2.06 Any agreements with "finders" or that purport to obligate the Company to compensate any person or entity in connection with a financing transaction

- ☐ 2.07 Private placement memoranda, investment letters, questionnaires, and other documents relating to any offering of securities of the Company
- ☐ 2.08 Copies, front and back, of all stock certificates and stock powers
- ☐ 2.09 List of any copies of closing binders of each and every prior equity financing (including debt convertible into equity)

3. Financial Statements and Audits
   - ☐ 3.01 Financial statements for the last three years
   - ☐ 3.02 Schedule of liabilities (contingent or otherwise) not reflected in the most recent financial statements
   - ☐ 3.03 List of any change in accountants and/or auditors since incorporation
   - ☐ 3.04 Copies of audit letters from counsel to auditors since incorporation
4. Taxes
   - ☐ 4.01 List of all domestic and foreign jurisdictions in which the Company remits sales, use, income, franchise, property, or other taxes
   - ☐ 4.02 Tax returns (federal, state, and local) of the Company since incorporation
   - ☐ 4.03 Reports filed and material correspondence with any and all tax authorities, including the IRS, since incorporation
5. Employees, Salaries, and Labor Disputes
   - ☐ 5.01 All collective bargaining agreements, employment agreements, offer letters, consulting agreements, severance agreements, noncompete or non-solicit agreements, change-in-control agreements and intellectual property transfer agreements, nondisclosure or confidentiality agreements to which the Company is a party, and list of any of the foregoing agreements currently contemplated or about to be entered into by the Company

- ☐ 5.02 Summary of labor disputes, requests for arbitration, organizational proceedings, grievance proceedings, and similar matters and history of recent union negotiations
- ☐ 5.03 List of all employees indicating each employee's division, title, function, industry experience, and earnings and whether each such person is an officer and/or director (or equivalent) of the Company
- ☐ 5.04 List of all employees terminated since incorporation and the reason for such termination; indicate whether each such employee has signed a release (and provide a copy of signed release)
- ☐ 5.05 Termination procedures, policies, and a sample termination letter

6. Employment Policies and Employee Benefits
   - ☐ 6.01 All personnel manuals, employee handbooks, and documents relating to employment policies and procedures
   - ☐ 6.02 Any affirmative action plan(s)
   - ☐ 6.03 Policies and practices regarding compensation for all employees not earning a straight salary (i.e., bonuses, commissions, overtime, premium pay, shift differentials, and so on)
   - ☐ 6.04 Policies for fringe benefits, perquisites, holidays, vacation, and severance pay
   - ☐ 6.05 Incentive, bonus, deferred compensation, profit-sharing, and nonqualified pension plans
   - ☐ 6.06 Employee health and welfare plans, whether insured or self-insured, including most recent summary plan description for each
   - ☐ 6.07 All Form 5500 Series annual financial reports and summary annual reports (including all supporting schedules and audit reports) for each employee-benefit plan described in 6.06 and 6.08

- ☐ 6.08 Each tax-qualified retirement plan and any related trusts or insurance contracts (as amended to date) and most recent summary plan description for each
- ☐ 6.09 Most recent IRS determination letter for each tax-qualified benefit plan

7. Financial Commitments
   - ☐ 7.01 All indentures, loan, and note agreements (whether demand, term, installment, or other) and line of credit arrangements, whether bank loans, industrial revenue bonds, mortgages, or other, and whether secured or unsecured, and all documents evidencing other material financing arrangements, including sale and leaseback arrangements, installment purchases, letters of credit, capital and leveraged leases, and receivables securitizations
   - ☐ 7.02 Summaries of compliance with the instruments described in 7.01 (including indication of whether defaults are presently anticipated for future periods) and all communications with lenders
   - ☐ 7.03 Guarantees for the benefit of or by the Company
   - ☐ 7.04 List of loans to or from securityholders, employees, officers, directors (or equivalent), or any of their immediate family members
   - ☐ 7.05 Contractual obligations relating to termination of employment
   - ☐ 7.06 List of all outstanding indebtedness of the Company detailing amount and effective interest rates of such indebtedness
   - ☐ 7.07 Schedule of all liens and encumbrances to which the property and assets of the Company are subject
8. Consents
   - ☐ 8.01 List of all material consents required to be obtained by or on behalf of the Company to complete the proposed transaction, specifying the name of the entity or

individual from whom consent is required, the agreements under which required, and the reason why such consent is required

9. Permits and Licenses; Compliance
   - ☐ 9.01 All material permits and licenses (including, without limitation, environmental permits and licenses) needed by the Company
   - ☐ 9.02 Description of any regulatory and compliance issues the Company has faced, currently faces, or anticipates facing (including, without limitation, FDA, HIPAA)
   - ☐ 9.03 Information related to potential regulatory or product liability claims or actions that the Company may face
   - ☐ 9.04 If applicable, written policies and guidelines regarding protection of personal health information and related privacy policies
10. Insurance
    - ☐ 10.01 All insurance contracts, including director-and-officer liability (or equivalent), automobile, general liability, environmental liability, key person (whether or not owned by the Company), and products liability; list of and summaries of insurance claims, disputes with insurance companies, or denials of insurance coverage that are currently pending or have occurred since incorporation; list of insurance claims paid against occurrence policies
    - ☐ 10.02 Workers' compensation documentation
    - ☐ 10.03 Vendor liability endorsements
    - ☐ 10.04 List of any time the Company has ever been declined for a policy or of any time an insurance company has declined to provide a key person policy requested by or on behalf of the Company (whether the policy was to be owned by the Company or not)

11. Litigation
   - ☐ 11.01 List of and status of pending and threatened claims, litigation, administrative, or other proceedings and governmental investigations involving the Company or, to the extent that they relate to performance of corporate duties (whether for the Company or any third party), any of the directors (or equivalent) or officers or relating to any product manufactured or distributed by the Company and list of counsel presently and previously handling such matters
   - ☐ 11.02 List of outstanding judgments or decrees against the Company and, to the extent that they relate to performance of corporate duties, any of the directors (or equivalent) or officers
   - ☐ 11.03 List of all consent decrees, settlement agreements, injunctions, and similar matters involving the Company and, to the extent that they relate to performance of corporate duties (whether for the Company or any third party), any of the directors (or equivalent) or officers
   - ☐ 11.04 List of all pending and threatened claims, litigation, administrative, or other proceedings and governmental investigations involving any key person (defined to mean any founder, officer, or director or key employee of the Company) during the last five years
   - ☐ 11.05 List of any and all bankruptcies and license revocations or suspensions or censures or prohibitions on involvement in the sale or trading of securities or commodities in which any key person has been involved if in effect during the last five years
12. Intellectual Property
   - ☐ 12.01 Patents, trademarks, service marks, copyrights, trade names, trade secrets, and other intangible assets owned or used by the Company (including domestic or foreign applications, registrations, licenses, and assignments)

- ☐ 12.02 Opinions relating to patents (including right to use, patentability, blocking patents, infringement, and validity) and opinions relating to trademarks (including registrability, infringement, and validity) and opinions relating to other intellectual property
- ☐ 12.03 List of all software programs owned by the Company that are (a) used internally by the Company in its business operations or (b) made available by the Company for use by customers
- ☐ 12.04 List of all software programs owned by third parties that are (a) used internally by the Company in its business operations (other than non-custom, mass-marketed software products licensed under a "shrink-wrap" agreement) or (b) made available by the Company for use by customers, indicating in each case the owner of and nature of the Company's right to use such intellectual property
- ☐ 12.05 License agreements relating to intellectual property under which the Company is licensor or licensee (including "shrink-wrap" software products to the extent related to the products developed by the Company) and list of any obligations to pay or rights to receive royalties
- ☐ 12.06 Documentation alleging infringement of third-party intellectual property by the Company or relating to alleged or actual third-party infringement of the Company's intellectual property
- ☐ 12.07 Secrecy, confidentiality, nondisclosure, and assignment of inventions agreements with employees, consultants, or independent contractors and list of any employees, consultants, or independent contractors not covered by such agreements
- ☐ 12.08 Written policies and guidelines distributed to employees regarding protection of proprietary items,

technical data, marketing data, or confidential information used by the Company in its business operations

- ☐ 12.09 Documentation relating to third-party development and testing of the Company's products, services, and proprietary products and information
- ☐ 12.10 List of any open source or community source code incorporated into any of the Company's software products or products under development
- ☐ 12.11 List of all liens and encumbrances on the Company's intellectual property

13. Property, Plant, and Equipment
    - ☐ 13.01 List of all real property currently and formerly owned by the Company
    - ☐ 13.02 List of all real property currently and formerly leased to or by the Company
    - ☐ 13.03 All leases and subleases regarding real property and material amounts of personal property leased to or by the Company
    - ☐ 13.04 All material agreements encumbering real or personal property of the Company, including, without limitation, mortgages, deeds of trust, and security agreements
    - ☐ 13.05 All material equipment leases involving the Company, including capitalized or financing leases
14. Environmental Matters
    - ☐ 14.01 All notices of violation or enforcement activity relating to any domestic or foreign environmental laws received since incorporation or otherwise unresolved at present
    - ☐ 14.02 All "potentially responsible party" notices, Section 104(e) (i.e., 42 U.S.C. §9604(e)) requests, or other documents relating to possible liability under CERCLA, on-site or off-site

15. Other Contracts

- ☐ 15.01 All contracts, agreements, or arrangements restricting the nature or geographic scope of the Company's business
- ☐ 15.02 All contracts, agreements, or arrangements between the Company and any officer, director (or equivalent), securityholder, or any of their immediate family members
- ☐ 15.03 All contracts, agreements, or arrangements between the Company and management or key personnel
- ☐ 15.04 All secrecy, confidentiality, and nondisclosure agreements between the Company and employees or third parties and list of any employees not covered by such agreements
- ☐ 15.05 All indemnification contracts, agreements, or arrangements for officers and directors (or equivalent)
- ☐ 15.06 All contracts, agreements, or arrangements between the Company and any of its subsidiaries or affiliates
- ☐ 15.07 All commission, brokerage, and agency contracts, agreements, or arrangements to which the Company is a party
- ☐ 15.08 All joint venture, partnership, corporate alliance, collaboration, and similar contracts, agreements, or arrangements to which the Company is a party
- ☐ 15.09 All executed closing documents relating to any merger, acquisition, or disposition by the Company (whether consummated or not)
- ☐ 15.10 All marketing contracts, agreements, or arrangements, including sales agent, representative, dealer, distributor, consignment, consultant, pricing, and advertising agreements, to which the Company is a party

- ☐ 15.11 All material supply, requirements, purchase, or sales contracts, agreements, or arrangements to which the Company is a party
- ☐ 15.12 All material licensing and royalty contracts, agreements, or arrangements to which the Company is a party
- ☐ 15.13 All government contracts, agreements, or arrangements to which the Company is a party
- ☐ 15.14 All contracts, agreements, or arrangements relating to the Company's securities to which the Company is a party, including, without limitation, subordination agreements, standstill agreements, stock option plans, forms of stock option agreements, and agreements pursuant to which the Company has agreed to issue or to register securities
- ☐ 15.15 All contracts relating to the operation of the Company's website
- ☐ 15.16 All other contracts, agreements, or arrangements that provide for the aggregate payment or receipt by the Company of $10,000 or more
- ☐ 15.17 All other material contracts, agreements, or arrangements

16. Miscellaneous
    - ☐ 16.01 All other documents and information that are significant with respect to any portion of the Company's business or that should be considered and reviewed by prospective investors in the Company

When Should All of This Data Be Uploaded to the Deal Room?

One of the biggest pitfalls in M&A is not having the data ready and available immediately. Once you get this far, you don't want the buyer to walk away. Don't blow it by not being ready.

If you are going down this path, you are either going to sell or merge the company, go public, or raise another big round of funding. In any of these scenarios, you are going to need a deal room, so make the investment and take the time to create one.

And get started early. By the time you hit due diligence, everything you need should be there, barring any documents that may need to be updated during a drawn-out period of due diligence.

If you aren't prepared, then you are going to look amateurish at best. At worst, you will look like you are hiding something. Neither of these perceptions is going to be attractive to buyers, especially when you are trying to get the highest possible price for your company.

Getting a head start on loading your deal room also means, quite simply, avoiding more pitfalls and mistakes that often crop up in due diligence.

While creating a deal room, it is common to discover that documents are missing or contracts and legal work that are missing signatures. You may find you need additional documentation. You'll also gain more of a buyer's perspective through this process and see potential gaps and areas for improvement that the buyer will notice. Finding this out yourself and taking the time to get things right before showing your information to buyers can make a huge difference in how smoothly due diligence progresses.

Validating Your Claims

Don't make claims that you can't back up.

It is relatively easy to create a great marketing and sales pitch. You can make all kinds of promises to investors to raise seed money. You can overpromise in ads to make sales and hope too many people won't complain or ask for a refund. You can also commission and create a fantastic pitchbook and exit presentation.

There may be some creative and artistic license when flaunting how great your company is, the strategic fit, and what's possible by merging your companies. However, anything to do with your financials, sales, asset values, partnerships, and product is going to be under scrutiny. All this has to be proven and documented.

The disclosure schedule will lay out exactly what data need to be provided to back up your claims, pitch, warranties, and representations. It will also lay out what you won't be required to prove.

If the potential buyer starts seeing critical information that is not lining up with your promises, you will be under even more scrutiny.

This is why due diligence and deal rooms are necessary.

The Dos and Don'ts During Meetings

Your due diligence process is probably going to be full of meetings.

Have an agenda for each meeting. This will ensure you are prepared. You need to time the meeting well to keep everyone from getting bored (or keep you from accidentally oversharing). You'll be making progress, rather than just burning time. Attendees will know what to expect, talk about, or take action on.

Listen twice as much as you speak. Build good rapport and hold engaging meetings that move the needle. Always keep in mind that you'll learn a lot more and grow your power in the negotiations considerably faster if you listen more than you talk. Resist the urge to speak as much as possible. Pause and take a few deep breaths before you have to speak.

You'll find listening much easier if you strive for objectivity and refuse to let emotions get the best of you. Being passionate and charismatic about your business and its strengths and vision is great. However, when you're in active meetings with the other side, you don't want to let any other emotions show. If you aren't careful, they will show through your body language (both during in-person and video meetings). They'll show in your voice and words over the phone. These are tells that professional negotiators on the other side will be looking for, and your emotions will be used against you—which is another great reason to have professionals in your corner to shield you.

Again, don't overpromise, make decisions, offer guarantees, or speak out without your lawyers, consultants, and board members. You are paying them to protect you. They are there to help you achieve the best possible outcome. They may even be the ones with the decision-making authority.

Managing the Flow of Information

Managing the flow of information is vital during due diligence.

Leaks of information or claims of a deal before one is struck can be incredibly destructive. They may break legal agreements. They might even be seen as fraud or at least attempts at stock and market manipulation. Both leaks and false information provided to the news or proclaimed to buyers could prove very expensive and may even cost you your role.

Leaks can affect the deal in a variety of ways. They can happen at many levels and for different reasons, or even by accident—and on both sides.

It's wise to throttle any information provided. There are sharks that will get into talks just to get inside data and tie you up. Typically, it is best to have your deal room fully loaded. You also want to be overprepared so that you don't slow down the deal. But that doesn't mean you have to provide complete access to every document and detail at once. You may open up more throughout the process as requested, without slowing things down, while preserving the integrity of your data and business as much as possible.

Using your VDR software, you can achieve this by creating different levels and areas of access. You can keep a tight grip on information by controlling access to sensitive documentation, throttling it, and tracking who has accessed it.

This book discusses the right time to share any potential thoughts of a merger or acquisition with different levels of your team and shareholders. Any other time is dangerous.

What to Look for in the Potential Buyer

You should be looking for several key factors in your potential buyer during the due diligence phase. You'll want to consider potential indicators of a good buyer and deal, as opposed to indicators of trouble or unscrupulous players trying to engage you and tie you up. The following sections help identify some of the things you should be looking for.

What Information Is The Buyer Asking For?

One of the factors you'll want to consider is the nature of the information your potential buyer wants. What information is the buyer asking for through disclosure schedules and other requests? What information is the buyer really trying to dig into? Is it in alignment with the buyer's stated goals and thesis for acquiring your company?

What Data Are the Buyer Looking At and When?

Using your deal room tools, you can see exactly who has accessed which documents, when, and how often. Does this activity line up with what the buyer is saying? Are the right people from the organization looking at the right documents and asking the right questions and in a logical order? Does all this align with the stated vision and intent? Are you seeing any quirky trends that could be red flags? Are people who should be looking at data relevant to a potential business merger involved? Or is someone just going through all of your IP and customer lists and neglecting data that would be more applicable to actually closing the deal on financially intelligent terms?

Making Excuses

You'll also want to make sure your potential buyer is authentically interested in the deal. Is everything the buyer is digging into becoming an excuse to ask for more information, to delay things, or to renegotiate the terms yet again? Or does it feel more like the buyer really wants to do the deal?

Efficiency and Honesty

A VDR with great tracking features gives great insight into the buyers you are courting. Are they working efficiently and transparently? Are they working through the schedules and data in an organized, swift, and thorough fashion? Or are they all over the place, claiming they can't find information you know they already accessed? The answers to these questions will tell you a lot about their integrity and even more about what they are going to be like to work with after the deal closes.

15

The Purchase Agreement

In tandem with due diligence, both parties also work on the official purchase and sales agreement. This is where it gets real.

The purchase agreement lays down all of the legally binding terms and conditions of the transaction, including all of the details and conditions for the closing and beyond.

This moves you from the LOI (i.e., "We might be interested in buying something if all the numbers work out for us") to "We're ready to sign the contract and close the deal."

There is a lot at stake here—not only a lot of money but also your team's careers, your customers, your credibility, your reputation with investors, and what you'll be committing to for the next several years.

The purchase agreement may be the single biggest and most impactful document you will ever sign in your life—probably the most significant until you sell another company. So, what should you be looking for in this document? Who should be helping you?

Of course, the lawyers are going to be heavily involved in this process. There's a good chance a lawyer will write up the original document, though there is more flexibility here than you might first perceive—and it always pays to be proactive.

Buyers may want to prepare and send the first draft of the purchase agreement, especially if they are active in M&A.

The first draft is the start of really meaningful negotiations. Multiple rounds of back-and-forth and refinement should be expected. In the name of preparedness, it's a good idea to strategize for this process.

However, just because the buyer typically makes the first offer, that doesn't mean the seller can't provide the first draft. In fact, there may be great advantage in doing so.

When you are given a legal agreement full of legal jargon and fine print, you psychologically take it as something official, something standard, and the way it is supposed to be. It has been designed this way, and we've all been programmed accordingly. (Think about NDAs, most loan documents, or all of the notorious privacy policies that no one reads.)

So when one side presents a sales agreement, the responsibility is immediately placed on the other side to try to make corrections, additions, and to negotiate edits to that document from a defensive position, and to do so while trying not to rock the boat of the overall "standard."

If the buyer sends you an agreement first, it is an uphill battle for you as the seller from the start.

If you can switch the dynamics from the beginning by going first, then the buyer has to take on the uphill struggle and is going to have to give to get.

For the small investment of grabbing a template and putting in a couple of hours of legal work to prepare the agreement, you may save a lot more in the long term.

How to Review the Purchase Agreement

Every M&A transaction is unique, however, most of the main components will remain the same.

It is vital to review your purchase agreement in full and in-depth. As tempting as it can be (and no matter how many companies you have bought and sold before), do not breeze over the fine print. Do not ignore the details. They can make all the difference in the ultimate outcome.

It should go without saying that all decision-makers who will be signing the document should be reviewing it in full, and your lawyers should be going over every line before you even consider signing a single page.

Take your time here. Don't allow yourself to be pressured into being rushed. Don't sign anything until you are comfortable that you understand everything and the implications. It's okay to keep asking questions (even the same questions) until you get it. The foolish people are those who don't ask and pay steep penalties later.

The main components of an M&A purchase agreement are discussed in the following sections.

The Definitions

Although you might think that the definitions are standard legal jargon, some financial terms and definitions may be open to flexible interpretation. This is especially true when it comes to financial adjustments. Be sure to go over these with your CFO and attorneys so that you understand what they really mean for the deal and your net and how they will influence the impact on your company after the closing in a merger.

Purchase Price and Payment Execution

What is the final price being paid for your company? How will the seller pay? Is it cash or stock? Are you financing any part of the purchase price? When and how will your company be paid?

What adjustments can affect the price? There may be adjustments to the price to ensure a certain level of working capital at closing, as well as the amount of debt on the balance sheet. Operating metric adjustments can be used by the buyer to ensure the target company is still performing and growing in the proclaimed direction when the deal is scheduled to close. If you are missing target metrics or there is a serious deterioration in the business, there may be adjustments or bigger issues.

Almost all M&A transactions have purchase price adjustment clauses. Of those with adjustments, working capital adjustments can be the most common.

Warranties and Representations

This covers what you are representing to be true about your business as the seller and anything you may be warranting for the future.

These representations and warranties (R&W) are a way for buyers to weigh risks and protect themselves, which leads to the next section—indemnification or compensation for claims that prove not to be true.

Typical representations in a transaction like this include these factors:

- Accuracy of any financial statements being provided
- Condition of physical property
- Existence of any legal liabilities (e.g., lawsuits, judgments, and so on)
- Details of employee contracts
- Status and amount of taxes

This section may also cover the disclosure schedule, detailing when the buyer will have access to all the information behind claims for due diligence.

R&W insurance coverage can be important here.

Indemnification

Indemnification is a mechanism that protects the buyer in the event warranties and representations are breached. This section of the purchase agreement lays out the details so that the seller is clear on and protected against claims.

These provisions can actually apply pre- and post-closing. Misleading claims that are discovered during due diligence and prior to closing may lead to due compensation for the buyer. The coverage for the buyer also extends out through the predefined "survival period."

This survival period can be anywhere from 12 to 24 months or longer for some items and some market conditions. The buyer may request monies be deposited into an escrow account for the duration of the survival period. This amount is negotiable.

This section should also lay out the minimum amount of any damage that can trigger an indemnification claim, as well as the cap, or maximum claim.

Note that some unscrupulous buyers will knowingly acquire a company in which they know the seller has misrepresented something, and then will use this clause to claw back a substantial cash refund on the purchase price. This is called *sandbagging*. Depending on the jurisdiction, it may not even matter if you can prove the buyer had advance knowledge of the issue at the time of closing. An anti-sandbagging clause could save you big with a risk like this.

Termination Provisions and Breakup Fees

This section spells out the conditions under which the transaction may be cancelled by either party (for example, if the buyer cannot obtain the expected financing or there is a breach of the agreement or misrepresentations in the process).

Obviously, by this point in the deal, both sides have made substantial investments of time and money. A great deal of goodwill and reputation may be on the line, as well as risk, after making disclosures and revealing data and other sensitive information. Breakup fees dictate who pays, and how much, in the event the transaction is cancelled by either party.

Closing Conditions

This section lays out the conditions that must be met prior to the deal's close and funding. It may include regulator approval, disclosures, assignments, debts being settled, verifications, shareholder approval, and proof of title to assets.

Covenants

The covenants mainly govern which actions each party must take, or must not take, during the transaction process. The most obvious of these is that the seller will continue to operate the business in good faith, with all effort to keep it running and growing as presented. Covenants can also cover issues such as incurring more debt or firing key employees, which may affect the value.

Terms and Clauses to Watch

Throughout the purchase agreement, there are a number of clauses and terms that you need to understand. The following sections examine some of the most common and important ones.

Jurisdiction

What legal jurisdiction governs this agreement and any disputes? Certain states are far more buyer-friendly than others and may routinely side a certain way in some clauses, such as anti- or pro-sandbagging clauses.

Stock Exchange Ratio

If your company is being purchased whole or in part with stock in the new parent company, what is the exchange ratio? The most likely stock price trends are worth taking into consideration between now and the closing, as well as how they can affect the net proceeds.

Asset Purchases

If your transaction is being structured as an asset purchase, everything that's included should be listed and inventoried in detail. If it isn't on the list, it isn't being transferred. And be sure to watch out for any mandatory repurchase provisions that could require you to buy back unnecessary or damaged inventory.

Earnouts

If part of the purchase price is being delayed or is subject to earnouts, what are the specifics? How long will you have to wait? What performance metrics will you have to sustain? What milestones are included? What provisions are in the agreement that will help or hinder you from meeting these payout requirements?

Make sure those earnouts are not completely out of your reach. Be conservative and push back if necessary. The buyer will try to put as much as possible on earnouts because it reduces for them the risk on the actual transaction.

Express Nonreliance

Express nonreliance, or "no other representations," inserts wording that indemnifies sellers from assumptions or any other factors not specifically included in the agreement. It states that the buyer is completely responsible for its own due diligence. You are not making any other warranties or representations beyond what is specifically listed in this section.

No-Shop versus Go-Shop Clauses

Will you be banned from shopping your company to other potential buyers during this period? Or will you be allowed? As the seller, you will ideally use the offer to go shop your business and create fear of missing out with other potential acquirers, which can help you push for higher bids. Just note that after signing this agreement, breakup fees could eat up a sizable portion of any higher bid you receive if you jump ship. At the same time, the buyer may want to lock you in and prevent you from soliciting other offers.

Pandemic and Epidemic Carve-Outs

Most contracts of all types provide provisions to carve out exceptions for material adverse effects, such as war, acts of terrorism, natural disasters, and acts of God. Post-COVID-19, expect epidemic and pandemic language to be specifically included, because it may be argued that these events do not fall under other, standard carve-outs.

Typical Purchase Agreement Outline

Purchase agreements often follow a fairly standard organization and structure. The following outline depicts what you can expect to see in a standard purchase agreement.

1. Purchase and sale of the purchased assets
   - ☐ 1.1 Purchase and sale of assets
   - ☐ 1.2 Excluded assets
   - ☐ 1.3 Assumed liabilities
   - ☐ 1.4 Excluded liabilities
   - ☐ 1.5 Purchase price
2. Representations and warranties of sellers
   - ☐ 2.1 Organization and power
   - ☐ 2.2 Authority to execute and perform agreements

- ☐ 2.3 Non-contravention
- ☐ 2.4 Capitalization; subsidiaries
- ☐ 2.5 Title to purchased assets
- ☐ 2.6 Financial statements
- ☐ 2.7 Legal compliance
- ☐ 2.8 Tax matters
- ☐ 2.9 Tangible personal property
- ☐ 2.10 Real property
- ☐ 2.11 Intellectual property
- ☐ 2.12 Contracts
- ☐ 2.13 Employees
- ☐ 2.14 Employee benefits
- ☐ 2.15 Litigation
- ☐ 2.16 Environmental, health, and safety matters
- ☐ 2.17 Insurance
- ☐ 2.18 Certain business relationships
- ☐ 2.19 Customers
- ☐ 2.20 Indebtedness
- ☐ 2.21 Restrictions on business activities
- ☐ 2.22 Absence of certain changes and events
- ☐ 2.23 Brokers' fees
- ☐ 2.24 Stockholder representative

3. Representations and warranties of buyer
   - ☐ 3.1 Organization of buyer
   - ☐ 3.2 Authorization of transaction
   - ☐ 3.3 Non-contravention
   - ☐ 3.4 Valid insurance of securities
   - ☐ 3.5 Brokers' fees
4. Covenants and other agreements
   - ☐ 4.1 Confidentiality; publicity
   - ☐ 4.2 Social media accounts
   - ☐ 4.3 Consents
   - ☐ 4.4 Name change
   - ☐ 4.5 Tax matters
   - ☐ 4.6 Employee matters

- ☐ 4.7 Covenant not to compete
- ☐ 4.8 Omitted assets
- ☐ 4.9 Agreement of stockholder

5. Indemnification
   - ☐ 5.1 Indemnification by sellers and recipients
   - ☐ 5.2 Indemnification by buyer
   - ☐ 5.3 Survival
   - ☐ 5.4 Limitations on indemnification
   - ☐ 5.5 Settlement of adverse consequence
   - ☐ 5.6 Third-party claims
   - ☐ 5.7 Sole recourse
6. Closing
   - ☐ 6.1 Closing
   - ☐ 6.2 Conditions precedent to obligations of buyer
   - ☐ 6.3 Conditions precedent to obligations of sellers
7. General provisions
   - ☐ 7.1 Representative
   - ☐ 7.2 Notices
   - ☐ 7.3 Succession and assignment
   - ☐ 7.4 No third-party beneficiaries
   - ☐ 7.5 Expenses
   - ☐ 7.6 Entire agreement; counterparts; headings
   - ☐ 7.7 Governing law
   - ☐ 7.8 Amendments and waivers
   - ☐ 7.9 Construction; severability
   - ☐ 7.10 Exhibits and schedules
   - ☐ 7.11 Arbitration
   - ☐ 7.12 Injunctive relief

Lawyers and the Purchase Agreement

Lawyers are the players in the deal whom everyone loves to hate. In sentiment, they often rank with car salespeople, real estate agents, and accountants.

The only time you love them is when they are saving you money, and this is probably one of the moments in your life when an attorney may add a lot of value and save you millions of dollars and untold amounts of stress.

Of course, the attorney will be well-compensated for his or her contribution, but if you know how to manage the attorney well and hire well, the person will prove invaluable.

Here are just some of the ways a lawyer can add value during this process:

- Helping you see clauses and negotiation points that can create the optimal outcome
- Spotting undervalued assets and strategies
- Saving enormous amounts of time
- Providing a valuable third-party buffer in negotiations (good cop, bad cop)
- Identifying areas of legal and financial liability and ways to protect against them
- Asking the what-if questions you don't know to ask
- Holding the other party responsible to its duties in the agreement
- Renegotiating terms
- Negotiating the best breakup if needed

Choosing the Right M&A Lawyer

There are a lot of things you should look for when choosing the right M&A lawyer for your transaction.

Experience Fit

Does the law firm have the right experience? Consider this not just in terms of the time in business or the volume of M&A transactions the firm has handled and closed successfully, but also in terms of the dollar range and domain you are in.

For example, does the firm specialize in $10 million to $100 million traditional business deals? Or $100 million–plus software startup transactions? Give them extra points if they know the buyer's M&A tactics. This kind of experience can make all the difference.

Global versus Local

If you are an NYC-based startup selling to an NYC-based corporation, then working with a local law firm that knows the market and playing field can be the way to go. But if you have international investors or are selling to a global conglomerate, you may need a firm with global expertise—one that understands the nuances in culture and paperwork between these jurisdictions.

Value for the Money

Lawyers for these deals are not going to be cheap. As with every role in your startup, you want to hire the best you can. Look at the returns you can expect to receive and evaluate the efficiency of more experienced experts. Don't get hung up on the hourly rate. Look at the total cost versus what being cheap could cost you.

Alignment

Alignment in philosophy here is far more important than the hourly rate or the law firm's name. You don't want an attorney who will tell you only what you want to hear. You want someone who is honest to a fault. You want someone who shares the same mindset on the best use of time and money and knows when to play hardball, rather than just getting it done and moving on.

Bandwidth and Priority

Does this lawyer and firm really have time for you? What level of priority are you going to have among their clients?

A famous attorney and firm may have its advantages, but that's not necessarily the case if you are their tiniest client and they are busy representing Oracle, Uber, and Google. Could it be more advantageous to find a less famous (but equally competent) firm? If you're their biggest client of the year, you can imagine the difference in attention and service.

Are there any conflicts with your time line? Is your lawyer due to head out to the other coast for a big case that could tie him or her up for months? Is your lawyer planning a vacation, having a baby, or counting down the days to retirement?

Dealing with Legal Counsel

Law firms have become a lot like franchises and realtors. You see the signs and hear the radio ads. If you are really lucky, you might get to speak with that big brand-name personality for about five minutes. They'll assure you they have you covered, but you may find out later that your case has been relegated to a junior staffer—after you hand over the big retainer. Make sure you ask the right questions and get to know the exact individual in charge of helping you.

It should go without saying that you shouldn't be communicating directly with the buyer or the buyer's legal team(s) during the purchase agreement process (at least not without your representation present). This is a big part of what you are paying your legal team for.

You will not only have your own M&A legal team but also your company's general counsel and your own personal lawyer.

M&A lawyers are deal-focused. They bring their expertise to the purchase agreement and getting through closing. Then, their job is pretty much done.

After this, your corporate general counsel may be involved with the integration and any post-closing issues. They are also the ones you'll go to if you have issues with your M&A team.

Your own personal attorney may be consulted on your obligations and risks in this process, as well as ensuring your rights are protected.

All of these legal professionals may be useful in breaking stalemates with opposing legal teams. Just watch your budget. Don't skimp on legal help, but make sure you find a balance in legal costs. Understand their roles, motivations, priorities, interests, and their mindset, and know when you need to reel them in and just get the deal finished.

16

Strategic versus Financial Acquisitions

NOT ALL MERGERS AND ACQUISITIONS are the same. Buyers can have very different reasons for wanting to acquire your company. These reasons can have a substantial effect on what happens:

- What your business may be worth to them
- What their expectations are in due diligence
- What factors are or are not important
- The terms that are up for grabs
- The transition

As with selling anything, the more you know and understand your buyer pool and the buyers in it, the better you can tailor your pitch and the more negotiating power you will have.

Different Types of Acquisitions

When it comes to acquisitions, you can generally think of them in two different ways: financial or strategic.

Financial Acquisitions

Financial buyers are looking at this purchasing opportunity as buying a financial asset—a stream of cash flow or return on their investment capital. Buying businesses is their business and form of investment. They may be more conservative in their offers. They are more likely to keep the current executive team in place for a longer period of time, provided the numbers are being met. Financial buyers may be more likely to use financing and debt to acquire your company. These transactions are more likely to happen later in a company's life cycle and typically the players going after this type of acquisition are for the most part private equity firms.

Keep in mind that if your startup has yearly revenues of less than $5 million, a financial acquisition may not be an option as your revenues will be under expectations of potential buyers.

Strategic Acquisitions

There can be a variety of strategic considerations when one company wants to acquire another. These buyers are typically already in your space in some way, or they want to be. They may look to own and operate you with some independence or absorb and merge your company as the parent. Their offers may be more aggressive, and it is more likely the leadership will be replaced, at least within the next three years, if not on sale. In addition to cash, strategic buyers will often offer stock in their company or a combination of both. Strategic acquisitions may happen far earlier than financial ones.

Reasons for Strategic Acquisitions

The financial reasons for making an acquisition are relatively clear-cut. The strategic reasons can be more varied and nuanced. The following sections examine some of the reasons for making a strategic acquisition.

Growth

Growth is what companies live and die by today. Sometimes it is easier to buy growth than to build it. This may be for customer acquisition, revenue, and even profits. Consider Facebook's acquisitions of Instagram and WhatsApp. Facebook as a social network is widely considered stagnant, or even declining in use, at least in the US. Although they paid large sums for these other two networks, they have brought crucial growth and relevance, which has supported its parent company.

Roll-Ups

It's not uncommon for startups to roll up their spaces by acquiring other startups ahead of an anticipated IPO or being acquired themselves.

Strength in Competition

Once startups prove a new market or product, they can face much bigger competitors moving in on them. By merging their forces, they can become much stronger and harder to dominate or run out of business.

Extending Control over the Supply Chain

Sooner or later businesses get to the stage where they see obvious advantages in controlling more of the chain in their industry. This may be for cost advantages and profit or control over quality, customer experience, and speed. Think about Amazon exiting deals with other last-mile delivery services and putting more of its own local vans on the roads. This may also apply to manufacturing, sourcing raw goods, distribution, and sales.

Legal and Regulations

In highly regulated industries, it can take years to get some types of licenses. Some licenses are even extremely limited or only available through bidding at specific times. Think about insurance, banking, or marijuana, in which the rules can be different for every state. It may be much faster and more efficient to acquire companies that are already licensed.

Entering New Geographic Markets

To continue growth, many companies will need to expand geographically to new markets. There's a lot more to it than just using Google Translate to put your website in a new language. There can be big cultural differences and nuances that take years to understand. Acquiring existing companies that are already there, know the language, and have relationships and a footprint can be much more profitable and low risk.

Buying versus Building New Products and Tech

Big companies aren't fast at innovating. It can be far more sluggish and expensive for them to test and grow new things than to simply buy something that a startup has already proven.

Economies of Scale

There are many economies of scale to be gained by merging companies. Both sides can benefit from lower costs, increased efficiency, and, in turn, more profitability.

Branding

Some smaller companies may have even stronger brands than their larger acquirers. Brands that have quickly gained brand recognition and love from customers can be great channels for larger ones. One example is Skype. Although the deal was positioned as an acquihire, it may have brought Microsoft a brand of communications much more attractive to many users than trying to develop their own.

Acquihires

Acquihires are a common way for other companies to acquire talent and ensure they have the best team in the industry or in a specific niche. If you are that good, they don't want to have to compete with you, and they definitely don't want you working for their competition. Given how much some corporations spend on recruiting, hiring, and onboarding, with few guarantees of success, buying your team may be a streamlined solution.

Removing the Competition

In some cases, M&A is about removing the competition. If you have a strong legal team that makes it look more expensive to try and sue you out of business and tie you up in court, or if it would take substantial capital risk to try to out-market you, then it may make more sense for them to buy you out than to compete against you. They can preserve those resources and their pricing to expand in other areas.

How to Know What Drives the Buyer's Motivation

How do you know what is driving the buyer's motivation to acquire your company or engage in the process?

In some cases, it should appear to be relatively obvious, though you also have to be on the lookout for unscrupulous players who just want to peek inside your company or tie you up. The better you know their drivers and levers, the more strategic you can be in presenting and selling your company and the more you can strategically negotiate to keep what you want and gain better value and terms for the pieces you are willing to let go.

For example, if you know they really just want to secure a specific technology, then you may be able to exclude and retain a product or IP that you think is actually more valuable and keep focusing on building that. It may make no monetary difference to them, but millions to you. Or if time is of the essence for them and their own plans, then agreeing to a faster closing can be bargaining power to justify asking for more stock in the deal.

Consider What Type of Organization the Buyer Is

One of the most obvious tells as to what is driving interest is what type of entity the buyer is—a private equity, or hedge fund, or family office—which may indicate the company is a financial buyer.

Or is the buyer a large global corporation, existing operator in your space, partner, or customer, which indicates the company is acting as a strategic buyer? If it is Google, IBM, Oracle, Cisco, or VMware, it is probably looking at your tech.

Ask

Just ask: Why is the buyer interested in acquiring your company? What is its company mission and vision? How does this deal fit into it? What does it see as the benefits of parenting or merging your company with it? Just as in fundraising, when meeting with individuals in early talks, ask what the thesis is that they are presenting to those they report to, and have to sell the deal to, within their own organization.

What They're Asking and Focusing On

Listen twice as much as you speak. What are the questions that the team members are asking? What are they focusing on in your business? What metrics, data, operation, or technological information are they most fascinated by? Is there any misalignment with their answers when you asked them?

What also might be driving them that they haven't announced? How do they react to certain statements you make about what you might do with parts of your business?

Their Track Record

What is this company's track record for negotiations and M&A activity? Is the company a highly active acquirer that is great at closing deals? Or is the company brand-new to this and doesn't have an organized process yet?

If the company has been acquiring other companies, what has been the stated purpose for those deals? How has it played out post-acquisition? Has it left them as separate business units? Dissected them, pulled out the technology, and left the rest for scrap? Has it kept on founders and key team members or not? Has it often resold companies quickly or shut them down?

Just as when evaluating and vetting potential capital investors in your company, it is wise to speak with others who have engaged with the company in the past to get the inside scoop. Talk to others they've done this dance with before. If deals didn't complete, why was that? If target companies turned down big offers from this acquirer, why did the founders and their boards choose to say no?

Of the companies your potential buyer did buy, how did the founders feel the acquirer did at being transparent up front? What was the due diligence process like? Did the company keep its promises after the closing? What was it really like to merge? What happened to its startups when it started integrating?

What's Happening with Its Business

Some general research may also hint at some of the buyer's motivations. What news is emerging about the company in the media? Have there been rumors of an IPO? Has it recently received sizable rounds of investment and acquired large amounts of cash to spend and put to work? What was the last round it raised, and when? Who participated, and what are their common strategies?

Is it obvious there are growth challenges for the company or competitors emerging ahead in tech or certain market segments? Is the company under pressure to quickly catch up?

Have big changes recently been underway in the market, future forecasts for the space, or the economy and methods of doing business?

Sites such as Crunchbase, LinkedIn, and Glassdoor may offer some interesting insights, too, such as recent hires, the direction of the company, reviews from previews, as well as existing employees or positions that have been closed.

Why Revenues Take a Back Seat on Strategic Deals

These different types of buyers and motivations can greatly influence what's important to them and what you should be focusing on improving and presenting.

In the case of financial acquisitions, it is largely about revenues, cash flow, and profitability.

Particularly with leveraged buyouts, the acquirer must make sure the income is there to cover the debt service. The buyer needs a minimum return, though there can be improvements made in performance later. The buyer is looking at the value of the business as is.

For strategic acquisitions, the priorities are quite different. When Facebook bought WhatsApp for $22 billion, WhatsApp's model was revenue coming from just $1 per download. Facebook did away with that and the subscription model, making it free for personal users. More than anything, it is now the data that appear most valuable.

Strategic deals may target companies with no revenues at all, or at least very lean incomes and profits. It is far more about what can be done with the company, people, product, and technology once it is in their hands, as well as what the target company can do for its existing business.

The company may be able to take a zero-revenue business and turn it into a billion-dollar producing unit in almost no time at all. Or it can double its user base instantly. Or it can eliminate costs and competition, which dramatically increase the profitability of the new parent company. It may even be a move the acquirer sees as vital for its own survival.

Although they say that companies are bought, not sold, there is certainly a lot your company can do to make it appealing and essential to buy and maximize the perceived and potential value. By understanding what's driving the buyer, you are able to model and present the right forecasts that demonstrate how valuable the merger and deal can be for the buyer in the right circumstances.

This doesn't mean that you shouldn't be building a profitable business with strong revenues and cash flow, though there can be other factors that are more important to certain buyers.

17

Ways to Kill a Deal

According to a study published by Baker McKenzie,[1] 83 percent of acquisitions fail mainly due to issues about people—in essence, the buyer and the seller not taking into account the importance of culture when pursuing a deal.

But there are additional common pitfalls to watch out for during the M&A process, which we will cover in detail in this chapter. As the entrepreneur and operator of the business, you ultimately want to avoid giving the buyer a reason to back out from the deal.

Make sure you consider these factors up-front so that all of the extra work, distraction, and stress is worth it.

Not Respecting the Buyer

Given everything that is on the line here, you should be finding a buyer whom you like, trust, and respect.

---

[1] https://www.bakermckenzie.com/-/media/files/expertise/employment/the-future-of-work-series--business-transformations-report.pdf?la=en

That can be hard. It may not be bulletproof. It is the buyer's job to sell you, after all. Still, if you want to be confident your acquirers will follow through on their promises to take care of your team, on the plans for your company and products, and really do their best to follow through on their offer, then it is worth taking the time to get to know them up front.

So when you begin the dance with the buyers, be sure you treat them with respect. Even at this level, it's about people. People can be emotional. Most aren't going to tolerate you being disrespectful of their time, position, and team members. You don't want to work with a business partner like that. Nor does anyone else. If there is no respect, don't expect anything else to make the deal work. Make sure you do the following:

- Show up to meetings on time.
- Do what you say you are going to do.
- Don't speak badly about your buyers behind their backs.
- Be courteous to their team members.
- Be civil in negotiations.
- Don't make them look bad.

Making Changes and New Demands

You can expect most buyers to make changes, make new demands, and try to renegotiate various parts of the deal throughout the process. That doesn't mean you should do the same thing or that they will tolerate you trying to renegotiate terms and make new demands during the process. Unfortunately, as with every part of building your startup, those that hold the gold get to make the rules.

This situation usually only arises if your team gets greedy or you completely overlook something up front.

The best way to avoid this temptation is to make sure your team is on board and be very clear on what you want and need.

Take your time before accepting a deal. Be clear on the outcomes you want:

- Price
- Multiple for your investors
- Transfer of technology, IP, and other assets
- Something for your team members
- Timing
- Your future freedom to work on other things

Think through your position on these things. Be sure you leave room to renegotiate. When acquirers want to change something to be further in their favor, then you already know what you can give and take and still get the bottom line deal you really want.

Lack of Commitment from the Team

Your team can kill the deal in a wide variety of ways.

The Board: Voting Power

If your board of directors and those with voting powers aren't on board with the deal, they can derail it fairly easily.

This can happen because they are trying to be greedy and don't think they are personally getting enough out of this deal. They may think they can get a lot more if an exit is punted down the road a few more years.

It could just be personal, if you haven't been getting along. Or, as investors, they could have other business reasons to hold back. Some may not agree with the vision of the acquirer and what the new business wants to do with the company.

A lot of this can be avoided by ensuring you are prioritizing alignment with investors and anyone else who is given shares and voting rights through fundraising rounds and recruiting. Nail that alignment clearly, and keep on reiterating and ensuring everyone is on the same page in terms of values, the mission, and the big vision.

Do this well, and the odds you'll be divided and can't agree on an exit or offer will be far smaller. People do change, but you can imagine how problematic this could be if you don't set out to accomplish this and just bring people in for ego and money.

Cofounders and the Executive Team

You will be relying heavily on your cofounders and executive team during this process. They may have almost daily interactions with the acquisitions team running the process on the other side.

If your people haven't bought into the deal, there are a dozen ways they can blow it. If they aren't all-in, then the way they treat the other team, what information they drop, the way they talk about your company and other team members, and how much they either help or drop the ball during the process can sabotage the deal.

If you are not all working as a cohesive team with the purpose of getting the deal closed, then you may need to smooth things over, use your strategic sales skills, and refocus everyone on the original vision, what's really important, and on the best move for the company now.

How You Communicate with Employees and Customers

The outcome of telling employees and customers about a potential acquisition or merger too early can be far more impactful than you imagine.

On the one hand, you may have learned to build your startup with complete transparency with your team. You may have shared everything, from the weeks when you almost didn't make payroll to the fact you were only a few weeks from going out of business. You may have shared all kinds of personal moments with your team members along the way.

Yet, some people advise that you should avoid telling your employees about a potential merger or acquisition until the last second. This may be more or less feasible, depending on how big your company and organization is. This issue is much easier to handle if you are working from home or if most of your team is thousands of miles away in another country. It's much harder if you are in one local office and new people have their fingers in everything. Some sellers may tell only their wider employee base on the day the deal closes and after the acquisition is official. Others are forced to tell them in advance because the acquirer wants to interview them.

Even if the deal never completes, employees learning about a potential M&A deal too early can wreak all kinds of havoc on your business. To really foresee and understand employee reactions, you have to put yourself in their shoes—not the way you think they should see it from your perspective, but how they truly see it from their position.

There are plenty of horror stories of what happens to employees in a merger or acquisition. They are going to be wrestling with a lot of uncertainty. They'll have even more doubts and concerns if the information doesn't come from you.

One of the biggest concerns is whether they'll still have a job and be able to pay the rent and provide for their families. Will they be assured a new job or ongoing role, and to whom will they report? What will happen to their bonuses, health benefits, perks, child care, retirement plan, and other types of compensation? All of a sudden, their minds are consumed with these unshakable thoughts. That can be hugely distracting, and it can affect their ability to work when you need everyone at his or her best, performing and making good decisions.

Rumors can spread that the people in the other company aren't great to work with. Perhaps one of your team members worked with them before and will be telling everyone else how bad it is going to be. That can lead to demoralization, apathy, and absenteeism. These things can spread quickly, like an infection, through the ranks.

Not only can you expect this to lead to low productivity but also mistakes in daily work and employees being short with other team members, vendors, and your customers. A quip on the phone or meeting can leak out.

Even in the best-case scenario that your team secures new employment contracts and the same level of compensation packages and job titles, it's unlikely you'll be merging with a company that has an identical culture and operating thesis. So now your employees face the prospect of going from a tight-knit group and exciting startup culture where they have an impact and can move fast to possibly the opposite. Then there is the mission. They bought into your company's mission. They wanted to work for you. Now what?

Unfortunately, most of the little information out there on acquisitions is targeted toward startup employees, and it's presented in a way that prompts them to take a defensive position. They are warned that no one cares about them as people in these deals.

If employees have stock, they are urged to get a lawyer of their own. This can also lead to employees shopping their stock to potential buyers and new funds.

One possible knee-jerk reaction may be that employees start calling recruiters and blasting out their résumés online to line up new jobs. Not only can this send out all the wrong signals for this deal and the company but also it can lead to competitors poaching some of your best talent at the worst moment for you.

All of these matters can create friction between you and your team. It can destroy the cohesiveness that got you to the deal and pit you against each other, possibly hurting the deal's chances. If the deal doesn't close, then your team may be a mess, and you can be in a worse position than when you started negotiations.

If customers and vendors have been treated poorly during the process, that can have a negative impact, too. They may choose competitors who are going the extra mile to win their business with great service. They may question whether the relationship is going to continue to be what they really want and need after this transaction.

This is clearly not a time when you want customer acquisitions, revenues, or operations to slow down or to have to spend a lot more of your personal time trying to mend bruised relationships. A lot depends on you here. It depends on how you lay out what's happening and what's next. It may depend on whether you've secured your employees new employment agreements and how you help them engage and get along with your acquirers.

During this period, everyone will be reacting to how you lead by example. Are you still showing up early and taking care of your team and working on the same growth plans as last month? Or have you changed and switched modes? Are you riding your employees harder than ever to pump up the numbers, sacrificing values by encouraging them to gloss over issues to make your company look better than it is, and then spending your days ranting or bragging about all the millions you are going to make from this transaction? (Although a few employees may get a tiny fraction of that money, will others lose their jobs?)

Ideally, you will have considered this moment right from the beginning, at least from the moment you begin fundraising and accepting outside investment. Part of your vision, mission, values, and culture that you continually iterate may include looking forward to this phase and the best outcome for everyone involved.

Frame it well in advance. Set expectations. Let your team know that although you can't promise anything (just like any other day in a startup), you will be seeking a great-fitting acquirer who is good for the mission and vision, who shares your values, and who will create the best outcome for as many team members as possible.

If you have properly prepared and taken your people's needs into consideration, when you do get to this point, everything will go far more smoothly.

Withholding Information

Withholding material information can be a very serious issue in M&As. I have seen many deals fall apart as a result. As the seller, you are warranting that all the representations you are making of your business are true and accurate.

Omitting information that can alter the numbers or value for the buyer in the future (if even only from their perspective) can become a big legal and financial problem, or at the very least, result in renegotiations in the middle of the process.

Your buyer is going to use auditors, accountants, and researchers to validate and scrutinize everything—just as you would with so much money on the line and the same legal responsibility to your shareholders and investors.

So if you left something out, they are going to find out. You can imagine how that may cause them to distrust you and want to dig deeper, and keep digging. It is far better to get any flaws out onto the table in advance. It will save you a lot of time and headaches.

Following are some of the common areas where acquirers discover information that wasn't disclosed.

Debts

Any existing loans, judgments, or other credit need to be disclosed. It can clearly change the value of the deal. Don't omit any new debt you have been applying for or negotiating. A new loan at the last minute can be an issue, too.

Ownership

Who are the owners, how many are there, what stock options have been promised? They want to know with whom they are doing business and who else has rights.

Accounting Issues

Many young startups are not very focused on accounting and taxes. What works for you in the early days of bootstrapping isn't going to fly when there are other shareholders involved or you are heading toward an IPO.

Legal Issues

Are there any pending lawsuits or legal settlements? Issues with regulators? What IP is really filed and owned (versus borrowed) or has the potential for copyright issues?

Liabilities

All liabilities need to be disclosed, and you shouldn't be taking on new ones during this process. It will create complications. Liabilities may include employment contracts, leases, and other financial commitments and operating expenses.

People and Customers

Are you losing any customers or team members the company thought were on board and were expected to be a part of the deal?

A good recipe to avoid a deal falling apart is to be humble at all times, to guide yourself with integrity throughout the process by delivering on your word, and to always be in communication with the relevant stakeholders so that there are no surprises.

18

Legal Considerations

What legal considerations should you be alert to when selling your company?

There are many legal considerations when negotiating an exit. You need to be aware of the potential risks and hurdles on your side, as well as what the perceived liabilities are for the buyer—plus, how to mitigate these risks and the adjustments a seasoned buyer and banker will demand in exchange.

Following are some of the most common legal questions and concerns when it comes to M&A.

Regulations and Regulators

Be keenly alert to any regulatory issues that could kill the deal. The issues may be big and obvious monopoly and antitrust issues or they could be industry-specific licensing issues. Real estate, insurance, health care, and communications companies can be particularly subject to governance. Be sure that ownership changes, especially across state borders, won't trigger legal issues that can cause the deal to blow up at the last moment.

Due Diligence and Assumed Liability

Generally, the acquiring company is going to be assuming the legal risks and liabilities of the target company when they close on the deal.

This, among the other factors in this list, is the reason due diligence can be so cumbersome, time-consuming, and painful. Acquirers want to have clarity on what exposure they may have, how much that may cost, and the liabilities they may encounter in the future.

This can specifically include any noncompliance issues or pending litigation. This may even take into consideration questionable practices that could become legal or major business issues, such as data sharing.

Intellectual Property

Intellectual property (IP) can be one of the most desired and valuable assets in a merger or acquisition. Acquirers are going to want to know exactly what is registered and protected, and how. They are going to be looking for potential legal issues and claims around that, whether they may be justified or not.

Working Capital

You want to ensure your business has adequate working capital after the closing, especially if there are any earnouts or escrows requiring specific performance in the years ahead. Acquirers should want this, too, unless they plan to dissolve the business. Look for financial adjustments to cover these capital and cash flow needs

Escrows

Your acquirer may request as much as 10 percent to 20 percent of the purchase price to be held in escrow. This is to cover them from unforeseen legal liabilities and costs or potential misrepresentations made by your company. This may stay in escrow for 12 to 24 months or longer.

Contracts

Much of your business's value may be tied to contracts, such as sales contracts and subscriptions, or critical contracts with suppliers and vendors. Acquirers will need to review these contracts for longevity and any clauses that may devalue them and your assumed business value.

Warranties and Indemnifications

Your paperwork will not only commit you to fully tell the truth and represent accurate facts but also will spell out the extent to which you and the acquirer are indemnified from future lawsuits and claims.

Stockholder Approval

Shareholder approval can be a legal issue. Know your stock's voting rights and power structure. Know your jurisdiction's laws on voting and what is considered a majority. Acquiring companies may also set even higher shareholder approval thresholds to minimize legal challenges later or to minimize risk after substantial cost and divulging of information. (The threshold can be as high as 90 percent or even 100 percent.) This is something you want to know as early as possible so that you can gauge how strong this deal is.

Noncompete and Non-solicitation Agreements

You and your team will likely be bound by noncompete and nonsolicitation agreements post-closing. Buyers don't want you to dump this company on them and use the proceeds to create an even better solution to the same problem or poach their staff. It may be possible to negotiate these clauses out, though typically it is a matter of how tight they are and how long they run.

Stock versus Asset Sales

There are several ways to legally and financially structure the sale of your company.

It can be an all-cash deal. It can be in exchange for stock. There are a variety of ways that the company and its parts are legally transferred and paid for as well. How do they differ? What can the impact or side effects of these elections be? Which is best for you?

Cash Deals

According to the *Harvard Business Review*,[1] the number one difference between these two forms of payment for your company is risk. All cash deals mean you are out and paid. Whatever happens next doesn't really affect your personal finances. You received your money, though you no longer probably have any say about anything that happens in the business. This scenario is, of course, a far larger risk to acquirers. All the risk is put on them and their shareholders. This can clearly affect pricing. The lower the risk for them, the more they are willing to pay. In a stock deal, you share the risk. If the merger or acquisition drags down your buyer's stock price, then you'll definitely feel it in your wallet, with the reverse true also.

Stock Purchases

There are two ways that stock purchases can work. You may be given stock (equity) in the new acquiring company or in the merged company that has combined its assets.

[1] https://hbr.org/1999/11/stock-or-cash-the-trade-offs-for-buyers-and-sellers-in-mergers-and-acquisitions

Asset Purchases

An alternative to the typical stock or cash purchase is a structured asset purchase. They're technically not buying the whole company or its stock. They are purchasing select assets from the company. This can be a more simplified transaction and can potentially mean needing less due diligence, not requiring approval by minor shareholders, and a quicker closing. The acquirer may also benefit from far less liability.

Fixed Value versus Fixed Shares

When you're being offered stock for your company, it is vital to differentiate between receiving a fixed amount of value in shares versus a fixed number of shares. Stock values will fluctuate over time, potentially making a huge difference in the net proceeds. It could be a big windfall or a massive disappointment. It's also worth asking whether the stock price is likely to rise on the news of a merger or acquisition or if it may tumble. Look ahead. What direction is the stock market as a whole likely to take in the near future?

How soon you can sell your shares can make a big difference, too. How long will you be locked in? At what dates will you be able to liquidate portions of that stock in the market? How good are you at timing the stock market? The future value of stock isn't just tied to the performance of your old company or the acquiring one. Stocks can be hyper-volatile. They rise and fall more on emotion than fundamentals. Consider this carefully and think about how to price in the risk for yourself if you do accept stock as payment.

Performance-Based Payments Post-closing

To balance risk and price for both sides, it is common to have a percentage of the sales price held to be earned or released over time—not just in escrow to cover unforeseen legal liabilities but also based on achieving and maintaining key performance metrics and milestones in the years after the closing. You may or may not be on board and in a leadership role to make sure that happens. Be sure the legal work clearly lays out what resources and control you will have to meet these criteria.

M&A Trends

Whether you will be offered cash or stock, or how offers are likely to be structured, can depend a lot on changing trends over time. If interest rates are low and money is cheap, then it can make more sense for acquirers to raise money and finance cash purchases of target companies. The same is true when companies have a lot of cash on hand. In other phases of the economy, cash is far more precious, and stock offers will dominate the M&A scene. Watch these trends and their timing if you are really set on one type of arrangement over the other.

Taxes

The top-line price can be meaningless if the terms and taxes eat you up. It's about what you get to keep. That's what is most important, at least when it comes to counting the cash, profits, and proceeds of an exit.

These different deal structures can make a substantial difference in how taxes are levied. Just like winning the lottery, cash typically triggers big bills from the IRS. You may easily be giving up 30 percent, 50 percent, or more of that lump sum almost right away, off the top. Stock and installment deals can spread out gains and how much cash you record in a given year over time. This can definitely help reduce tax exposure, especially in conjunction with other smart multiyear tax strategies.

Taxes can change over time, too. Elections and big shifts in political power can sometimes create dramatic changes in tax rates, what taxes apply, and what shelters may be available. Keep this in mind and evaluate what this could mean for your net by the time you close the deal.

Don't underestimate the value of a great CPA and tax expert. Be sure to get personalized advice for your unique situation before making any assumptions.

Post-closing Company Performance

If continuing your startup's mission and seeing your company and team continue to flourish after the sale or merger is important to you, then how the deal offer is structured and how you are paid can be a significant signal of what's next.

Will acquirers be more motivated to put in the work and investment to make your venture thrive if they pay precious cash or they've borrowed heavily to purchase you? If they are just buying your assets or haven't committed resources for the longevity of the business in the paperwork, is it more likely they'll break it up?

If they fail or end up struggling financially themselves, what legal issues may arise? What liabilities may they try to throw on you and your cofounders?

Your personal connection to those on the other side of the table, synergy in work cultures, vision, and values, can all play a role in future performance and legal issues. But just like any partnership, it also pays to address these legal issues in advance, in writing. What jurisdiction will govern disputes? What resolutions are available?

Buying Companies That Are Not Incorporated

There can be a variety of unforeseen glitches when selling a young startup. Many of them can center on the articles of incorporation and initial stock.

Not Having Incorporated the Business

Some groups of cofounders take way too long to debate, file their company, and get off the ground as a result of worrying about small details. Other entrepreneurs, either in a rush or feeling overconfident, just steam ahead, either without incorporating the business or just registering online in a few seconds and never giving another thought to their articles of incorporation or that side of the business. That may not seem to have any negative impact on just getting to work and creating a thriving venture, but it is a fundamental part of a transaction when it comes to selling the business. If you don't have an actual business that is incorporated to be sold, then you may be limited to just selling the assets. That can still create a great outcome, but it may short-sell the true potential value of a strategic acquisition. It's always better to use an attorney and incorporate from the beginning, with the end in mind.

Incorporating Less-Desirable Destinations

You'll find common threads among most of the companies that big acquirers buy, as well as in where they are incorporated themselves. Delaware is the most popular state in the US for its privacy and tax laws. Nevada and Wyoming are also top choices. Other states can be far more expensive.

Not Issuing Founders' Stock

Having failed to assign or issue founders' stock in the company at the beginning can bring a variety of issues when it comes to raising equity capital and selling the business. The value of the stock will change over time, and there can be less clarity from a legal standpoint on who owns intellectual property, as well as differences in the time before founders can sell their stock.

Other Issues

Other legal issues can arise from neglecting this side of the business if meetings and formalities are ignored and personal and business funds are commingled, leaving questions over the legal protections and validity of the corporation. Taxes can certainly be affected as well. Even typos in the registered company name or forgetting to renew the corporation can become expensive mistakes that can derail a business sale, even after having received an LOI and seeming just days away from the closing.

Although there are cheap DIY options, good attorneys will more than earn their fees for taking care of these details for you.

Liens and Encumbrances

Startup businesses often take on a lot of different types of debt and encumbrances in the early days of the journey, typically without considering the real impact on a sale and the value of the company.

These encumbrances can include the following:

- Business credit cards
- Business loans and lines of credit
- Debt and credit facilities for operations
- Merchant cash advances
- Equipment and vehicle financing
- Commercial real estate loans and leases
- Pending or existing legal judgments

These are forms of liens on the business and future income. Some may also come with personal guarantees from the founders, which can lead to their personal assets being pursued in a default.

When cleaning up your business, paperwork, and finances to prepare your company for sale, you may want to eliminate a lot of debt. Don't leave yourself without any cash or financial runway. It may be more appealing with less debt and higher net profits. Your future acquirer may also have access to superior financing at much lower rates if they do want to finance anything.

If you can't or prefer not to settle these debts in advance, then make sure you learn what the consequences are in selling the company as is.

If there is a significant change in ownership, can the new buyer assume the debt according to the terms of these agreements? Will a sale accelerate the balance of any debt being due? What easements or encumbrances may there be on any real estate that could make a substantial value difference for the new owners?

It can be confusing to pick the best type of currency to accept for your startup. You also need to know how to structure all of the legal. And, of course, you have to decide to whom to sell your startup. This is a big part of the reason I went on to start Panthera Advisors after exiting my own startup.

19

Closing the Deal

You've made it through the LOI, the bulk of the due diligence process, and you've negotiated the final sales and purchase agreement. What's the next step to actually get the deal closed and get money in the bank so that you can move on to the next stage for yourself, your team, and the company?

The Anatomy of an M&A Deal Closing

Buying and selling a business isn't like one-click Amazon checkout. An M&A closing is probably the most complex and time-consuming type of sales transaction there is.

Even after you've hashed out and negotiated the final, definitive purchase and sales agreement, there may still be things to work out.

You can have a closing simultaneous with signing the purchase agreement, but in the vast majority of mergers and acquisitions deals, the closing is a multistep process

1. Closing conditions
2. Signing final agreements and documents transferring ownership

3. Final financial adjustments
4. Transfer of funds, disbursements, and paying taxes
5. Integration
6. Solving post-closing issues

Once all closing conditions are met, the actual closing can be scheduled. Key factors at this stage can include regulatory and shareholder approval.

Closing Preparations

The deal isn't closed until everyone has signed *every* document and funds are transferred.

You can expect your lawyers to take the lead here in reviewing the closing documents and overseeing the required signatures and compilation of signed paperwork.

Although your legal team will go through every detail, with so much on the line, it's in your best interest to read every word of the documents, no matter how tempting it is to gloss over the legal terms and fine print and simply take the final documents as "standard." If something is inaccurate, be sure you have it corrected before signing, no matter how much pressure you are under. Failure to do this can prove to be extremely expensive, whether due to representations and warranties, financial adjustments, or changes in earnout provisions.

The final documents that constitute the closing will include the actual transfers of ownership of stock, intellectual property, corporate assets, accounts receivable, and any other related assets. This is when you should also be signing employee contracts, noncompetes, and so on.

Closing Times and Locations

Where closings take place can vary. If your office is down the street from your acquirer, then it is possible you'll go to their offices and sit in a conference room to tackle the stacks of paper that need to be signed.

But often, you may be on the other side of the country or even the world. It may not be practical or possible to get everyone together at the same time. Ever since COVID-19, virtual closings have become more common. Virtual notaries and digital signatures are the norm for just about everything today.

Speed to Closing

Speed to closing is one of the top concerns for sellers in M&A. The faster you can close, the less risk of the buyer backing out. It also reduces the risk of occurrence of any material events that could devalue your company or the stock you are promised.

Because time is so important, choosing a buyer who is capable of and committed to closing quickly is often more important than the top-line price being offered.

Buyers know that seller fatigue from drawn-out closings can often pressure sellers into giving up more concessions and negotiating points to speed up the closing process. It isn't uncommon for sellers to give up double digits in price discounts to just get the deal done.

The following are the four most common negotiation points that often hold up deals and derail closings:

- Disagreements over working capital funding
- Disagreeing over the length of management team commitments
- Negotiating noncompete clauses for management teams
- Inability to agree on reps, warranties, and covenants

Unfortunately, over 50 percent of all deals can still fall through before closing, even after purchase agreements are signed.

The faster you can resolve these negotiation points and get closing conditions crossed off the list, the better.

Accounting and Taxes

Taxes are unavoidable. It's not how much you make on the top line, but how much you get to keep when it comes to the financial part of exiting your business. Key factors here include the following.

Understanding the Difference among Types of Sales

Different types of transaction structures can mean proceeds have different classifications of income for tax purposes and ongoing corporate taxes for all entities involved. Is it a stock or asset purchase? Will you be paid in cash or stock? Will the buyer be financing its purchase? The type of business entity being acquired and how it has elected to be taxed to date can also make a sizable difference. Be sure you understand these nuances of the deal and how these structures can help, or they will yield far less than hoped. Of course, different structures can also help the buyer optimize different bases for its own future tax gains or losses. Your interests are usually at odds here.

Rights to Pre-closing Tax Prep and Filings

The purchase agreement should lay out who has the right to prepare and file taxes for the pre-closing period, as well as who will be responsible for or have control over managing any post-closing tax audits for this period. The more control you have as the seller, the less you'll pay in taxes, and the lower your risk of losing more in future audits.

Tax Indemnifications

Buyers will want you to indemnify them from any unexpected tax liabilities that can arise after the closing. If you are footing the bill, then they will have little motivation to fight any audit issues. Have your lawyers carve out as many exceptions to these indemnifications as possible.

Tax Reform and Changes

Don't overlook the potential for tax reform and changes before the closing. This can be especially important around times of crisis and new transfers of government with new, incoming presidents and political parties coming to power. Big changes can occur in taxes on foreign income and assets, as well as changes in corporate tax rates, personal income tax brackets, and tax credits. These can all have a substantial impact on the net deal. Look forward and keep likely changes in mind.

Understanding Personal Tax Liabilities

A huge windfall from the sale of a business can create a lottery-sized personal tax bill. Although the money for your pocket may not be the main driver, it pays to understand the tax consequences and what they mean for you personally. After all, you are using up a lot of time and energy on a transaction like this. It should be worth your while. If you dismiss this factor, you will probably be incredibly shocked at what taxes will take out.

Secure yourself a great CPA and tax strategist to help you assess your liability and the money moves you can make to minimize your tax bills and maximize your net gains for the long term.

Post-closing Financial Adjustments

Even after all the negotiations over price, the price paid is still subject to accounting adjustments. The adjustments can be due to changes between the agreement date and actual closing and after the closing.

The vast majority of M&A deals include post-closing purchase price adjustment provisions. More than half can include adjustments based on more than one metric, such as the following:

- Differences in company value, finances, and earnings before closing
- Net earnings from earnouts and performance-based payouts
- Adjustments in working capital figures
- Escrow releases for indemnification, reps, warranties, and so on

If there is a negative change, you as the seller may have to wire funds back to an account of the buyer's choosing.

Any dispute resolution needs should follow the clauses in the purchase agreement and may require an independent accounting firm to be involved.

Closing Checklist

There are a lot of documents and action steps needed for getting your transaction closed, and you'll need to coordinate these with your legal, financial, and management teams. These include the following items:

- ❒ Final purchase agreement
- ❒ Escrow agreement
- ❒ Transaction services agreements
- ❒ Bill of sale
- ❒ Assumption and assignment agreements
- ❒ IP assignments
- ❒ Lien and title searches for real property
- ❒ Transfer of deeds for real property
- ❒ Seller resolutions to authorize the transaction
- ❒ Buyer resolutions authorizing the transaction
- ❒ Disclosures
- ❒ Government approvals

- ❒ Third-party approvals and consents
- ❒ Judgment and lien searches
- ❒ Resignations of officers and directors
- ❒ Preparation of seller share certificate transfers
- ❒ Preparation of flow of funds memorandum
- ❒ Transfer of purchase price to seller's bank account
- ❒ Creation and distribution of press release announcing the transaction

Wrapping Things Up

After all of the rush and stress, the actual closing and seeing the funds show up in your account can often feel very anticlimactic.

Make sure you plan for some well-deserved downtime after the transaction is complete. You'll need it. Any partner and kids you have will definitely deserve your extra quality time after this sprint.

If you will be involved in the transition of your company and integration after the closing, you'll need to regroup and refocus on the next stretch of the journey. Be sure all members of your existing team who are making the crossover with you are on the same page. Make sure they understand how any performance pay applies to them and the new protocols for doing business. Everyone should know the goals and metrics you need to hit and when.

Whether you are part of the integration or not, it pays to stay alert to potential post-closing disputes and issues. You'll also want to keep an eye on the escrow account and the countdown for the release of any funds still tied up.

There is probably more than enough money at risk in escrow to warrant keeping an attorney on retainer to monitor these funds and their disbursements.

In the case of post-closing disputes or claims by the buyer, make sure you are well informed about the mediation and resolution mechanisms in your agreement. This means you need to be familiar with the institutions that you are agreeing to oversee a potential mediation or arbitration in the event of a dispute with the acquiring company so that you are not putting yourself in a difficult situation.

20

Transitioning to a New Phase

THE DEAL IS FINALLY CLOSED. Now it's time for a whole new phase for your life and business.

Unless you sold your company for all cash up front, you will likely go through an extended stint working on your business as an employee of your new owner. This is typically a legal part of the purchase and sales agreement under earnout or revesting clauses.

As mentioned before, hopefully, you've negotiated some much-needed time to vacation. You'll definitely need time to decompress and destress after all of the intensity and anxiety during the sprint toward your exit.

Use it to spend some time recovering, reenergizing, and clearing your head. Recoup as much of the time you lost as you can with your family, friends, and others you care about after all of the crazy hours you've invested over the past few weeks or even years. Chances are you'll be back at it harder than ever soon enough. Don't let this opportunity slip away. Invest time at home and travel if you can. Enjoy a few great experiences afforded by all of your hard work and payout.

Vesting and Revesting

Earnouts and revesting clauses can take different trends over time as markets change, depending on your industry, stage, and acquirer intent.

They all have the same main theme, which is delaying a substantial portion of the purchase price and proceeds to the buyer. For sellers, this de-risks the transaction, maximizes their cash flow and returns, and enables them to act much earlier to take advantage of your assets. They aren't paying most of the top-line purchase price until certain conditions are met. That may be milestones or time based.

There can be some advantages for sellers, too. Accepting these terms and conditions in your deal may enable you to sell for dramatically more. Just make sure you can stomach them, stick with it, and deliver. Or you can end up with extra stress, legal issues, and far less money than you anticipated.

Earnouts

Earnouts give sellers the opportunity to earn more based on fulfilling certain metrics or achieving specified milestones.

How common and significant earnouts are will vary over time, by industry, and depending on the market and economy. The American Bar Association[1] says it expects earnout clauses to become more common and make up a larger percentage of payouts in the aftermath of COVID-19. Expect earnouts to be present in more than 30 percent of deals and to make up nearly half of the purchase price. For life sciences startups, earnouts may be found in more than 60 percent of M&A transactions. They may also last longer. (Consider an average of 24 months at the beginning of 2020 to three to five years post-COVID.)

[1] https://www.americanbar.org/groups/business_law/publications/blt/2020/09/anatomy-earnout/

Business Law Today[2] reports that 11 percent of earnouts are greater than five years, and that in 30 percent of cases, earnouts are indefinite or the time line is "silent."

Founders also need to factor in the risk that they cannot meet objectives, especially when there are extreme circumstances, market shifts, and cycle turns that may affect the ability to deliver on the goals and criteria for earnings.

Here are the most common earnout metrics:

- Revenues
- Earnings
- Regulatory milestones

Earnouts can also be tied to these criteria:

- The launch of new products
- Sales volume/units
- Expansion

These two groups can also be combined to make earnouts more complex.

Another major factor to consider is what happens to earnouts when your buyer is acquired by someone else during this period. It is probably more common than you think, and it can make getting paid far more complicated. Ideally, as the seller, you want your earnout payout to be accelerated in this scenario.

Perhaps most important is the ability to work and operate in a way that enables you to achieve these earnouts after the closing. You might be surprised to learn that in 98 percent of deals, buyers may make no written agreement to run your business in a way that helps maximize payouts. Very few agreements even promise the

[2] https://businesslawtoday.org/2020/08/anatomy-earnout-era-covid-19-best-practices-designing-earnouts-avoid-disputes/

company will be able to run as it used to or that there is any fiduciary responsibility of the acquirer.

The following are indicators that you may be in for a rough time:

- Combining business units
- Combining your products with theirs
- Selling off material assets
- Laying off employees and management

Good signs to look for include these:

- Providing money for capital expenditures
- Hiring more
- Providing your company with access to their resources
- Keeping the businesses and accounting separate

How dispute resolution is laid out can potentially be a sign of intentions as well.

Revesting

If you did your homework and applied appropriate vesting strategies in putting your own startup together from the beginning, this should not be a foreign concept for you.

The vesting period is a safety measure that enables those with stock options and shares to earn their stake over a period of time. When you launch a startup, the last thing you want is several founders or key team members being given significant amounts of equity, only for them to quickly disappear, not put in any work, and then get just as much financial benefit as you do after you've sweat, bled, and burned yourself out for years to make your company succeed.

You can understand that in an M&A deal, the same concerns apply to your new acquirers. They don't want you to just toss them the hot potato while you run for your bunker with all of the proceeds.

In contrast to earnouts, revesting is time-focused. It is about proving what you said and the value over a period of time. It can also be about locking you and your top talent up so that you aren't out there competing against them and devaluing their investment.

When you are given stock in the new company for your sale, a percentage of this won't be vested, or really become yours, until the vesting period or its milestones are up. There may be some tax advantages to spreading out these payments, though these rules are constantly in flux. This revesting period may last one to four years or even longer, though you may receive lump sums at various milestones and preset dates throughout this period.

For example, if you and your cofounder sold your startup for $100 million, and 60 percent went to your investors, then you and your cofounder may each get $5 million per year for the next four years, provided you stick with the new organization. Or, if you can shorten that, you could get $10 million at closing and another $10 million at the end of the first year after the acquisition.

How you structure and word the value of these payouts and earnings can make a big difference, too. Are you being given a fixed dollar amount? Or is it a certain number of shares, which could be worth dramatically more or less by the time they are fully vested?

Sometimes revesting is sold to entrepreneurs as an easy gig—just showing up to clock in for a couple of years. Of course, any true entrepreneur isn't cut out for that. You're not designed to tolerate just checking in for mindlessness every day for any period of time. Being locked in those golden handcuffs can feel like a fate worse than death for those who survive on doing something: doing something meaningful, having an impact, and having a purpose.

Hopefully you will have the ability to really do some meaningful work and keep creating progress and results and see your mission being fulfilled during this period. However, it can depend a lot on the written terms of your transaction and the reality of the promises made after the fact. Having chosen your buyer well will make all the difference for this phase of the journey.

What you don't want is to be at odds with your new bosses and their ethics and then wind up walking away from millions or billions of dollars. That's what happened to the founders of WhatsApp, when Facebook had different ideas about what to do with their data. The two cofounders had to walk away from $1.3 billion in payouts because they simply couldn't take being there for another 12 months.

If you do find yourself in this situation, then it is worth attempting to negotiate an early buyout. That may have to come at a discount. Or if the integration and new asset just isn't working out for the acquirer, then you may be able to buy some of it back.

On the bright side, this could be an incredibly empowering period during which you enjoy learning many new things and making new connections, which may prove pivotal in your next startup venture.

Post-acquisition Integration

Post-merger integration is where the rubber really meets the road. This is especially true if there are earnout and revesting provisions holding your money ransom, though it is just as important if you want to see your company flourish, your mission progress, and your employees see their jobs sustained.

Of course, integration can also be the toughest part. It is where the majority of M&A deals sour. Focus and expert management is critical here. Getting the pre-closing agreements right is going to greatly determine how this goes and how hard it is. The rest is going to be hustling to make it happen and practicing the art of diplomacy on many levels.

Start Early

Integration can't be an afterthought. It can't be something you wait until after the closing to address—at least not unless you don't care if it is successful or has a fighting chance of working.

Integration shouldn't be addressed only in financial negotiations. Plans and efforts should already be in progress in advance of the closing, as much as possible.

Leading the Integration

Integration requires great leadership. You can't do it all yourself. As the seller you only have so much power, and there can be some natural headbutting because of your position. Your companies will hopefully be able to form a strong and balanced integration team. You may also want to employ a change management expert who knows how to handle these challenges and weld companies together.

A third-party expert can also greatly help eliminate power struggles and "us versus them" mentalities—at least while people get used to the new power structures. Then, make sure teams are clear that the challenges of this integration are what they need to work together to solve, instead of competing against each other.

Create a Time Line

Draft a time line with your acquirer for how you'll merge your businesses together, as well as for the next steps for your operations.

Create a Detailed Action Plan

Just as with launching your startup, know the big things that need to be achieved over the months ahead, while maintaining a very short and focused list of your next one to five action steps:

- Deciding how much autonomy your company will have or not
- Creating a new organizational structure map
- Handling new employee contracts and benefits transfers
- Managing layoffs
- Merging and replacing technologies

- Combining communications
- Implementing new accounting systems

Document a System

Bain[3] reminds us that it is important to document and systemize. Create a repeatable process. It probably won't be your last M&A deal. At certain points in the future, you will probably be on one side of the table or the other.

Culture

Integrating teams and culture is the most critical component here. If people aren't working together, then they are working against each other. There is enough competition out there, without competing against your own organization internally.

Culture is probably the number one factor—not just in integration but for the success of business in general. Although each office and country may have its own culture or variations and spin on this culture, there can be only one company culture going forward. It is probably not going to be the same scrappy, small startup culture your company came in with.

However, if you make sure there is a good match in cultures even before you begin seriously talking about an M&A deal, then things should work much more seamlessly. Despite location and size differences, you may be surprised to find how well things can mesh together, especially with people of the same caliber and with the same ethical values.

Getting team members together as much as possible and empowering them to bond on a personal level can go a long way toward a smooth integration as well. Getting together off-site can be a

[3] https://www.bain.com/insights/the-renaissance-in-mergers-and-acquisitions-how-to-make-your-deals-successful/

fantastic way to achieve this. In times when this isn't possible, consider how to get them together in smaller groups online in as human an interaction as you can.

Looking Forward

Remember, although there may be a lot to keep you busy during this phase of the journey, it's just a pit stop. Keep your eyes open for what's next.

Use this time to learn, to forge new connections, and explore new things. Consider what you can take from the experience to kick-start a new venture of your own—one even better than the last one. Compile what you've learned from this transaction and the integration efforts so that you structure your next startup with the end in mind and enjoy an even better ride.

21

The Emotional Roller Coaster during Acquisitions

In 1969, Elisabeth Kübler-Ross wrote the book *On Death and Dying*. The book explores the five stages of grief: denial and isolation, anger, bargaining, depression, and acceptance. In the book, Kübler-Ross provides examples and stories illustrating how imminent death and the aftermath affect everyone around a person who is in the process of dying.

The book offers a framework to help people who are in the grieving process. Believe it or not, getting your company acquired often leads to a grieving process. The grieving process emerges because ultimately everyone associated with the company will never experience the business as it was prior to the acquisition closing. Significant change can trigger grief.

Yet, selling your startup can be one of the most exciting moments you'll ever experience in your lifetime. It can certainly be one of the most exhilarating and pivotal. But it can also be one of the most trying and stressful periods you'll ever have to go through.

There is very little information out there for entrepreneurs about the M&A process, and even less is good-quality information.

It's almost impossible to find info and stories on the mental and emotional aspects of this roller-coaster ride.

Entrepreneurs rarely open up about the reality of launching and building a startup, fundraising, and the many daily failures and trials involved.

To my knowledge, at the time of writing and publishing this book, there really hasn't been any substantial documentation or disclosure about this part of the founder's journey, though I've been able to pull back the curtain through interviews on the *DealMakers* podcast with real founders who have sold their startups for millions and in many cases billions.

There will be plenty of learning and challenges in this short phase of your journey. When you understand how the process relates to anxiety, isolation, and depression, you can better navigate your path to acceptance and happiness.

This chapter isn't meant to discourage you from having your company acquired. Rather, I want to empower you, by providing a road map to get through the process so you know what to expect. Entrepreneurs don't just run on financial capital—they also run on emotional capital. For that reason, being conscious of your state of mind and the triggers behind it is key.

Anxiety

You may get an initial buzz of excitement at the thought of being able to sell your company. Big numbers and big partnerships can be alluring.

Then, once it starts becoming real, panic can begin to creep in, and a string of factors can trigger a period of anxiety, which will last until the deal is closed and money is in the bank.

If you haven't studied ahead, then not knowing the steps in the process and being mentally prepared for the roller coaster is going to bring additional anxiety. Educate yourself, and it will be much easier.

Understanding the Process

Having a good overview and visibility of the process will bring some peace, because you will know what needs to happen every step of the way until the deal is closed. The following sections look at a lot of the parts of the process that can affect your emotions.

The Terms and Conditions

As the initial flirting begins to turn into real talk, anxiety about the terms can set in.

The top-line price, valuation, stocks versus cash, and whether you'll stay on under the new parent company or you'll be free to go out on your own are just the most basic aspects to consider.

There may be questions about some of the intellectual property and products you don't believe your acquirer will use or continue. You may want to find a way to continue the missions they were created for, such as carving them out of the deal.

You may care deeply about what will happen to your cofounders, employees, and early investors. Will those who believed in you at the beginning get a good multiple on their investment? Will your cofounders get a fair payout and be set on a great path for their individual goals? Will those employees who helped make everything happen and sacrificed comfy jobs at steadier companies be kept on by your acquirer? Will they be given good roles, salaries, and benefits?

Due Diligence

How intense and lengthy the due diligence will be can depend on your stage of business and how much there is to go through.

This process can involve various teams digging into your legal work, finances, and data. You may have dozens of people on-site looking through every document and even talking to your customers throughout this process.

In many instances, I have seen teams locking themselves up in a hotel room with the potential acquirer and going through documents together for weeks.

This will all happen while you are desperately trying to keep up your business's performance.

Renegotiations

The final terms of your deal can look a lot different from the initial offer. Expect to feel so exhausted talking about negotiations and hashing out different terms and clauses that you almost don't care whether the deal closes by the end.

Tough acquirers will find all types of reasons to renegotiate and change things. Stay strong and maintain focus. Don't let them take the necessary energy away from you.

The Sprints

When you are closer to a deadline concerning the LOI or the final agreement, you should expect to sleep less. This will be a very stressful time as things will be negotiated over and over again between lawyers. You need to remain calm, trust the process, and avoid your frustration from getting in the way of getting the deal done.

The Silence

For weeks, dozens of people can be all up in your business. Then, one day, everything goes quiet. No phone calls. No one showing up in your office. Complete silence.

If you are not expecting it, it will freak you out and make you feel isolated and anxious. There can be a variety of reasons for this. It doesn't mean the deal is dead.

Be patient. The last thing that you want at this point is to sound desperate. The buyer may use that against you and negotiate you down on the terms. A good way to set up expectations and keep this from happening is by setting up weekly check-ins.

Anticipation

Anticipating the closing can be nerve-wracking. You don't know if it is going to happen and you need to clear out your office and announce the next stage of your life, or it is going to fall apart and you'll be working more furiously than ever to make up for the lost time.

You'll survive this best if you can emotionally detach yourself from the outcome. The best deals happen when you are completely unattached to the outcome of the deal.

The Calm after the Storm

After all the mayhem, the deal closes, funds are wired, and everything goes still. If you aren't clocking in at your parent company on Monday, then things can seem eerily quiet. This dramatic change of pace can take a few days to adjust to.

Sharing the News with Employees

Typically, when it comes to acquisitions, you want to avoid sharing details with employees until the deal is closed to avoid any leaks that could jeopardize the deal getting done.

During the process, you will only be sharing what is going on with the leadership team and with other key employees who could play a critical role to close the deal.

When the deal is finally closed, it is a tough moment to deliver the news to employees. Many of them will probably not own stock in the business, and they may be disappointed by the potential changes ahead.

To be effective here, you just want to be yourself and authentic. Don't sugarcoat it, as people will see through it and create a disconnect. Just share it the way it is and acknowledge them for everything they have done for the business.

Share with employees the joint vision with the acquirer and where things are heading. You were excited about this deal so you should be able to convey that to them and get them equally excited about what is coming.

A majority of mergers and acquisitions fail primarily because leaders ignore the emotional needs of their employees. Employees are a key component to the deal being a success. That is why effective communication and improving the employee experience is critical—especially if there is an earn-out component and your employees will determine the potential outcome of the deal.

Depression

Although this is probably something you'll never hear from an investment banker or acquisitions team, the M&A process and hangover of selling your startup usually involves a grieving process. This is especially true for selling your first company, and even more so if you swore you'd never sell it.

In these cases, separation and loss are very real. If you aren't prepared for it, the days after closing the deal can be far more depressing than you imagined, even if you made out pretty well financially in the exit.

I can tell you from personal experience and real conversations with other highly transparent founders that this loss can often feel as real as any other.

If they say partnering up with cofounders and investors to give birth to a company is like a marriage, then selling it can feel like divorce or giving away your baby—or at least, sending them off to kindergarten for the first time, hiring that first babysitter, or shipping them off to college.

The money comes in a distant second. You are severing ties with your baby and putting it in someone else's hands, where you have no control.

Think about this for a second. You were used to the fast pace and having full control over the execution of the business, and now, all of a sudden, things go on cruise control and you are reporting to someone else.

This is something you've been supremely passionate about. You care about the people you've lived with and fought alongside in the trenches every day for years. Many of those employees sacrificed their paycheck or professional journey because they believed in you and the vision of the business. Often, the business was your main mission in life.

You wake up the next morning and maybe you can't even call in to check on them. You can't go to the office. You have to sit in the bleachers and watch from a distance without being able to go on the field.

This can leave a real void in your life for a while, one that can come back or continue to be a nagging factor in the back of your mind until you get through these next two phases of the roller coaster.

There's a lot of advice that's easy to throw around, but it may not immediately make you feel better. Understand that this is just part of the ride, and it is temporary. The best ways to beat it and speed through it is to talk to others (family, peers, and mentors), remember the good parts, look to the next phase, and accept it.

Acceptance

The sooner you can get to this stage, the better it will be for you.

If you have mentally prepared for the emotions that will arise, and you have trained yourself to be more objective and think of the big picture in advance, you'll get to acceptance faster.

Accept that you may feel a real loss. Accept the emotions that come with that. Yet, also be clear with yourself that it is done. You sold your company. For better or worse, it is a done deal. Who knows—one day in the future they may want to sell it back to you at a discount.

For now, the only thing you can be grateful for is the great ride you had. Enjoy the present, and plan an even more fulfilling future.

After all, it may not even be your second or third startup that is your greatest work and accomplishment. It may be your fourth or fifth.

Happiness

If you've equipped yourself by reading this book, you've hopefully achieved a profitable outcome. Your investors achieved a great multiple that will make them want to give you money again in the future and refer you. Your team has gone on to grow professionally, and many of them were financially well rewarded for their participation and loyalty. Your customers are being taken care of even better than you could, and the mission continues to prosper.

You also received a game-changing financial reward from this exit. The money may not be the main thing, though you can count it as a win and a confidence booster, and you've set up your family to be comfortable.

You now have the luxury of operating from a place of doing what you are really most passionate about rather than for your own finances.

Even if you didn't walk away with a penny, you can be happy for the incredible learning experience and the chance to go on to do something even better.

Overall, there seems to be three general scenarios for exiting founders to take consider when taking their next step. If you've already been thinking ahead, you may already be rolling into your next startup. That's great. Why wait? That's the first scenario.

The second scenario is that the terms of your merger or acquisition required you to stay on as an employee of your new owner. This is called the vesting period when you need to stay for a period of time in order to receive all the cash or stock that was promised to you with the deal.

Some entrepreneurs have loved the learning experience the process opened up for them in large-scale companies such as Google, Facebook, or Microsoft. It's given them the chance to learn from a bunch of smart, new people and to see how things are done at a different level.

Invariably, however, the honeymoon period comes to an end. Some make it through the full vesting period, others pull the emergency eject cord much sooner. They crave being back in a startup, going fast, and building something of their own again.

Keep in mind as well that during the vesting period you are working 9 a.m. to 5 p.m. as opposed to being always on duty, like you were before the acquisition. This enables you to have a full-time job with an income stream while you are crafting, as a side project, what could be your next startup.

The third scenario is to finally take that much-needed time off. It's a smart move. It's a chance to really decompress, while you can. A short window where you can relax and focus on things outside of the office for a while. It could be a long time before you get that kind of luxury again. Stay present, and you may find it to be one of the best rewards of building a successful startup.

Periods of decompression are often spent heading off to a cabin away from the city, traveling the world to meet other entrepreneurs, finding new ideas, gaining new perspectives, and spending time with family.

Some dream of early retirement and finally being that ever-present stay-at-home parent. That may last six weeks or six months. Sooner or later, your family is going to beg you to go do something and stop hovering.

You may even do a stint of some angel investments of your own.

Go learn and do all the things you might not have time for if you've been neck-deep in a new startup—because once you've tasted entrepreneurship, you'll never want to stop.

The good news is that the roller-coaster ride of anxiety, depression, and resigning yourself to acceptance of your new circumstances is short-lived, and after experiencing the void, you'll be on to your next project (if you haven't already planned it out).

Knowing this is all coming, line up some great new projects and goals for this period, and cling to the excitement of being able to tackle them to get through the tough days.

Ultimately, you want to be able to gain emotional intelligence. This will enable you to control your own emotions and help manage the emotions of others (particularly when it comes down to preventing any reactions that could disrupt what is a very fragile process).

Now you know there is a silver lining on the other side of the clouds.

Glossary

Industry lingo and terms are always changing. It's important to stay up-to-date on M&A terminology, even for the entrepreneur who has completed successful fundraising rounds and scaled a company.

Use this quick glossary to refresh and update your knowledge of the common terms you'll encounter during the M&A phase of the journey. It will prepare you to efficiently navigate meetings and offers; deepen conversations with buyers, bankers, and lawyers; and can go a long way toward securing a better outcome.

acquirer: An organization or company buying or making an offer to buy a business.

acquisition: The act of purchasing a controlling interest in another company or its assets.

angel investor: An individual investor who invests his or her own capital into early-stage startups.

asset sale: A type of acquisition in which the acquirer buys all or most of the target company's assets.

assets retained: Any assets that the owner is able to keep after the closing of the transaction.

balance sheet: A financial statement listing the liabilities, assets, and capital of a business.

book value: The value of a company, calculated by subtracting intangible assets and any liabilities from the company's total assets.

breakup: When the buyer and seller do not complete the deal and one party withdraws from the transaction.

bridge financing: Shorter-term financing used to bridge cash flow gaps or carry a venture until preferable long-term financing can be secured.

burn rate: How much money a company is burning through on a monthly basis—typically used for pre-revenue startups or those not yet profitable.

business broker: A professional or company that specializes in connecting corporate buyers and sellers and helping to facilitate the transaction.

CAPEX: Stands for capital expenditures. An investment in a new asset or a means to improve the life of a current asset.

capital gains: The profit made on selling an asset or stock.

capitalization: How a company is capitalized; the mix of debt financing, equity, and classes of stock.

capitalization rate: A method of calculating the rate of return on an investment.

capital structure: How a company funds its operations and growth.

cap table: The capitalization table listing the company's outstanding and issued securities.

carve-out: An exception to a rule, provision, or term of an agreement.

cash flow: The net cash flow a company has after expenses.

CIM: The abbreviation for confidential information memorandum. The CIM is a document outlining a business's history, financials, and considerations for investment and is typically used to pitch a company to potential buyers.

convertible debt: A vehicle for fundraising that begins as debt and can be converted to equity at a later date or on the occurrence of a certain event.

covenants: Contractual agreements and clauses included in the purchase agreement, mandating or prohibiting certain actions.

DCF (discounted cash flow): A method of valuing businesses using the present value of future cash flows.

deal room: A physical or virtual room in which sensitive data on a company are stored and shared among the buyer, seller, and their representatives. Also known as a data room.

deal structure: How the deal is structured—specifically including whether it is being acquired for cash, stock, or a mix of both.

defensive merger: A merger of two companies designed as a defensive strategy to protect against competition or hostile takeovers.

dilution: The diminishing effect on ownership due to issuing new securities or debt being converted to equity.

discounted cash flow (DCF): A method of valuation using the present value of future cash flows.

dividends: Payments made to the owners of securities.

due diligence: The process of validating, verifying, and investigating the claims and assets of a target company by an acquirer.

earnout: A clause or provision in the purchase agreement that requires the seller to earn part of the sales price through future performance after the closing of the transaction.

EBITDA: Earnings before interest, taxes, depreciation, and amortization.

equity: The owned interest in an asset after deducting all liabilities.

exit strategy: The plan or options a company has for exiting or liquidating its equity.

financial acquisition: An acquisition purely for financial and investment purposes.

founder: An individual who participates in the creation of a company.

goodwill: Intangible value created by loyalty, reputation, and perception.

horizontal integration: The merging of companies in the same lines of business. Often used to expand, reduce competition, or create a larger entity.

hostile takeover: An offer that is unwelcomed by the target company.

institutional investor: A large corporate entity with substantial amounts of capital to invest on behalf of its investors.

integration: The merging or absorption of one company into another.

intrinsic value: The value of a company determined purely by calculating the value of its tangible assets.

investment banker: A professional or firm that specializes in raising capital, trading securities, and matching corporate buyers and sellers.

IOI: Stands for indication of interest. This is a first-step document from the potential buyer to a seller indicating interest in making a purchase.

IPO: The abbreviation for initial public offering. An IPO occurs when a company transitions from being a private to a public company and has its shares publicly traded on a stock exchange.

joint venture: A partnership of two or more companies through which they may finance or acquire the acquisition of a target company, often by creating a third entity.

lead investor: An investor who commits to be first in a round of fundraising and often ends up making the largest investment and leading most of the due diligence and documentation.

leveraged buyout: Also known as an LBO, this is a financed acquisition, often collateralized by future protected revenues.

liquidity: Available liquid cash, or the ability to quickly convert an asset to cash.

LOI: The abbreviation for letter of intent. An LOI is a nonbinding letter from a potential buyer to the seller outlining the main points of a potential deal and purchase.

M&A: Mergers and acquisitions.

M&A advisor: A professional or firm that consults and advises private companies and may act as a broker to assist in positioning and preparing for a sale, connecting the company with the right buyers for the optimal outcome.

majority interest: A controlling interest in a company, typically holding at least 51 percent of votes.

noncompete: A contract or clause preventing the signer from competing against the buyer of his or her company.

no-shop clause: A clause in the purchase agreement that prohibits the seller from soliciting additional bids for the company during the due diligence phase.

P&L: A profit-and-loss statement, typically reported annually and year-to-date and often audited.

pitch book: Also known as the memorandum in which a company lays out the basics of their business and the opportunity to acquire it.

pitch deck: A presentation in slide format, pitching the company and the opportunity to invest in it.

restructuring: The rearrangement of the liability and asset structure of a company.

reverse takeover: When the new shares issued by a listed company and given to an unlisted company are so great that the private company gains control of the public company.

road show: The series of presentations and meetings made to investors or potential acquirers for a fundraising or exit event.

SEC: The abbreviation for the Securities and Exchange Commission, which regulates and enforces securities laws and stock exchanges.

shark repellent: Amendments to company bylaws that make it less appealing for a hostile acquirer.

stock exchange ratio: How much of the acquiring company's stock will be received in an acquisition.

strategic acquisition: An acquisition that offers the buyer strategic benefits beyond any direct return on investment from the target company on its own.

supermajority amendment: A provision that requires a very high percentage of shareholders to approve M&A transactions or make other major decisions.

tangible assets: Physical assets such as equipment, real estate, and cash.

target company: A company that an acquirer is targeting to buy.

term sheet: The document outlining the key terms of a transaction.

valuation: The agreed-on value or process of valuing a company for sale.

vertical integration: When an acquirer buys a target company that is part of its supply chain.

voting rights: The right of a shareholder to vote and make decisions in relation to their percentage of ownership of a class of stock.

About the Author

Investor, serial entrepreneur, best-selling author, and cofounder of Panthera Advisors, Alejandro Cremades (alejandro@pantheraadvisors.com, @acremades, www.alejandrocremades.com) has become one of the most notable names in the startup ecosystem.

Since immigrating from Europe to the US, Cremades has become a leading advocate for entrepreneurs, a pioneer in the startup fundraising space, and is considered by some as the voice of startup M&A.

Cremades has been named to the Top 30 Under 30 lists of GQ, *Vanity Fair*, and *Entrepreneur* magazines. TechCrunch has heralded Cremades as one of the influencers shaping the NY tech scene.

Today, Cremades is a high-level connector and one of the most active dealmakers in the startup space.

Cremades was born in Madrid, Spain, to parents Bernardo and Leticia, who knew education was integral to their son's success. His mother, in particular, was so focused on his academic work that she waited 15 years to tell him he'd been drafted to play for the premier soccer club Real Madrid.

After graduating with his law degree from Universidad San Pablo CEU in Spain, he hopped on a flight to New York City with his brother and immediately fell in love with the Big Apple.

After receiving his master's degree in international business and trade law from Fordham Law School, he joined the law firm of King & Spalding. There, he worked on one of the largest investment arbitration cases to date, *Chevron v. Ecuador* (with $113 billion at stake).

In 2010, Cremades cofounded RockThePost with Tanya Prive (who is now his wife). RockThePost acquired CoFoundersLab, FounderDating, and 1000 Angels, and became known as Onevest.

Onevest became one of the largest online communities supporting entrepreneurs. The site was ranked as one of the best for entrepreneurs by *Time* and *Forbes*. By the time Onevest was acquired for millions of dollars in 2018, the platform had over 500,000 active registered members.

During this period, Cremades was invited to the White House Champions of Change program. As an early player in the JOBS Act, he was called to testify to the US House Committee on Small Business on his position on equity crowdfunding and the future for businesses.

Cremades's first book, *The Art of Startup Fundraising*, distills his experiences and expertise in startup fundraising for entrepreneurs. Published by John Wiley & Sons, with foreword by *Shark Tank* investor Barbara Corcoran, the book lays out how funding works, as well as strategizing rounds, pitching, identifying the right investors, and closing the deal. This book has been named one of the best books for entrepreneurs by *Inc.* magazine, and labeled by Book Authority as one of the best fundraising books of all time.

The Art of Startup Fundraising has received rave reviews from the late CEO of Zappos and author of *Delivering Happiness*, Tony Hsieh; Tim Draper, vice chairman of Dun & Bradstreet; Jeff Stibel, executive director of the Angel Capital Association; Marianne Hudson, CEO of the Family Office Association; Angelo J. Robles, and more.

After exiting Onevest, Cremades launched his website AlejandroCremades.com. On the site, he shares weekly information and updates on the fundraising and M&A deal space. The site is also his online home for Inner Circle, a live coaching experience that has helped entrepreneurs systematically raise successful rounds of financing ranging from $200,000 to $100 million.

As a speaker, he has been called to important stages in Latin America, the US, and Europe, and he has guest lectured at the Wharton School of Business, Columbia Business School, and NYU, and at the Angel Summit.

More recently, Cremades created the *DealMakers* podcast. With nearly 2 million downloads since launch, it is among the top-five business podcasts. *DealMakers* has featured 300 of the world's top founders and investors, and offers unique insight into how the most successful entrepreneurs raise money, build, scale, and exit businesses, and find winning ideas.

Cremades's latest venture is Panthera Advisors, in partnership with M&A superstar Michael Seversen. In just three years, Panthera Advisors' fundraising and M&A advisory service aided clients in hundreds of transactions around the world, including one of the largest Series A financing rounds in history.

To find out more about Mr. Cremades, visit AlejandroCremades .com.

Index